BE DETERMINED

#1318

Wie   #1318

Zion Chapel

Be Determined

WARREN W. WIERSBE

Chariot VICTOR
PUBLISHING
A DIVISION OF COOK COMMUNICATIONS

Victor Books is an imprint of ChariotVictor Publishing,
a division of Cook Communications, Colorado Springs, Colorado 80918
Cook Communications, Paris, Ontario
Kingsway Communications, Eastbourne, England

Copyediting: Jerry Yamamoto, Barbara Williams
Cover Design: Joe DeLeon
Cover Photo: Tony Stone Worldwide

Library of Congress Cataloging-in-Publication Data

Wiersbe, Warren W.
   Be determined / by Warren W. Wiersbe.
     p.   cm.
   ISBN 0-89693-071-8
   1. Bible. O.T. Nehemiah — Commentaries. I. Title.
BS1365.3.W54 1992
222'.807 — dc20

                             92-13327
                               CIP

---

3 4 5 6 7 8 9 10   Printing/Year 01 00 99 98 97

CONTENTS

Dedicated to

Birne Wiley
and the
Missionary Tech Team
Longview, Texas,

choice servants of God, who, like Nehemiah,
are determined to build the walls to the glory of God.

PREFACE

Speaking of Nehemiah, Charles Spurgeon said, "We are not called to govern, as he did, with an iron hand, but we ought to be equally inflexible, decided, and resolute for God, and for His holy will."

In other words, God calls us to *Be Determined!*

God's work has never been easy, and in these last days it is getting more and more difficult to serve. The enemy is hurling his ammunition at us as never before and is setting his subtle traps where we least expect them.

But the same great God who enabled Nehemiah to finish building the walls of Jerusalem will enable us to finish our course with joy and accomplish the work He has called us to do. There is no reason to quit or even to despair!

In my estimation, when it comes to leadership, Nehemiah stands with Old Testament heroes like Moses, Joshua, and David. It has done my heart good to study this book afresh and learn from Nehemiah the secrets of resolute leadership and successful service. I trust that reading these chapters will increase your own determination to serve God faithfully and finish your ministry with joy.

Warren W. Wiersbe

A Suggested Outline of the Book of Nehemiah

I. Concern — 1
   1. Information — 1:1-3
   2. Intercession — 1:4-9
   3. Intention — 1:10-11

II. Construction — 2–3
   1. Authority — 2:1-10
   2. Investigation — 2:11-16
   3. Challenge — 2:17-20
   4. Assignments — 3:1-32

III. Conflict — 4–6
   1. Ridicule — 4:1-6
   2. Plots — 4:7-9
   3. Discouragement — 4:10
   4. Fear — 4:11-23
   5. Selfishness — 5:1-19
   6. Compromise — 6:1-4
   7. Slander — 6:5-9
   8. Threats — 6:10-16
   9. Intrigue — 6:17-19

IV. Consecration — 7–12
   1. The people — 7:1–12:26
      a. Checking the genealogy–7
      b. Teaching the Word–8
      c. Confessing sin–9
      d. Making a covenant — 10:1–12:26
   2. The walls — 12:27-47

V. Cleansing — 13

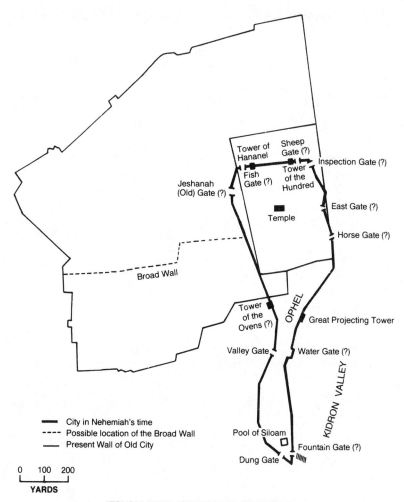

JERUSALEM IN THE TIME OF NEHEMIAH

Tower of Hananel
Sheep Gate (?)
Inspection Gate (?)
Fish Gate (?)
Tower of the Hundred
Jeshanah (Old) Gate (?)
East Gate (?)
Temple
Horse Gate (?)
Broad Wall
Tower of the Ovens (?)
OPHEL
Great Projecting Tower
Valley Gate
Water Gate (?)
KIDRON VALLEY
City in Nehemiah's time
Possible location of the Broad Wall
Present Wall of Old City
Pool of Siloam
Fountain Gate (?)
Dung Gate

0   100   200
YARDS

From *The Bible Knowledge Commentary,* Old Testament, © 1985 by SP Publications, Inc. Used by permission.

Does Anybody Really Care?

The worst sin toward our fellow creatures is not to hate them, but to be indifferent to them: that's the essence of inhumanity."

George Bernard Shaw put those words into the mouth of the Rev. Anthony Anderson in the second act of his play *The Devil's Disciple*. The statement certainly summarizes what Jesus taught in the Parable of the Good Samaritan (Luke 10:25-37); and it rebukes all those who fold their arms complacently, smile benignly, and say somewhat sarcastically, "Ask me if I care!"

Nehemiah was the kind of person who cared. He cared about the traditions of the past and the needs of the present. He cared about the hopes for the future. He cared about his heritage, his ancestral city, and the glory of his God. He revealed this caring attitude in four different ways.

1. He cared enough to ask (Neh. 1:1-3)

Nehemiah was a layman, cupbearer to the great "Artaxerxes Longimanus," who ruled Persia from 464 to 423 B.C. He is identified as the son of Hachaliah to distinguish him from other Jews of the same name (Neh. 3:16; Ezra 2:2). Nehemiah means "The Lord has comforted."

A cupbearer was much more than our modern "butler" (see Gen. 40). It was a position of great responsibility and privilege. At each meal, he tested the king's wine to make sure it wasn't poisoned. A man who stood that close to the king in public had to be handsome, cultured, knowledgeable in court procedures, and able to converse with the king and advise him if asked (see 41:1-13). Because he had access to the king, the cupbearer was a man of great influence, which he could use for good or for evil.

That Nehemiah, a Jew, held such an important position in the palace speaks well of his character and ability (Dan. 1:1-4). For nearly a century, the Jewish remnant had been back in their own land, and Nehemiah could have joined them; but he chose to remain in the palace. It turned out that God had a work for him to do there that he could not have accomplished elsewhere. God put Nehemiah in Susa just as He had put Esther there a generation before, and just as He had put Joseph in Egypt and Daniel in Babylon. When God wants to accomplish a work, He always prepares His workers and puts them in the right places at the right time.

The Hebrew month of Chislev runs from mid-November to mid-December on our calendar; and the twentieth year of Artaxerxes was the year 444 B.C. Shushan (or Susa) was the capital city of the Persian Empire and the site of the king's winter palace. No doubt it was just another routine day when Nehemiah met his brother Hanani (see Neh. 7:2), who had just returned from a visit to Jerusalem, but it turned out to be a turning point in Nehemiah's life.

Like large doors, great life-changing events can swing on very small hinges. It was just another day when Moses went out to care for his sheep, but on that day he heard the Lord's call and became a prophet (Ex. 3). It was an ordinary day when David was called home from shepherding his flock; but on that day, he was anointed king (1 Sam. 16). It was an ordinary day when Peter, Andrew, James, and John were mending their nets after a night of failure; but that was the day Jesus called them to become fishers of men (Luke 5:1-11). You never know what God has in store, even in a commonplace conversation with a friend or relative; so keep your heart open to God's providential leading. I attended a birthday party one evening when I was nineteen years old, and a statement made to me there by a friend helped direct my life into the plans God had for me; and I will be forever grateful.

Why would Nehemiah inquire about a struggling remnant of people who lived hundreds of miles away? After all, he was the king's cupbearer and he was successfuly secure in his own life. Certainly it wasn't his fault that his ancestors had sinned against the Lord and brought judgment to the city of Jerusalem and the kingdom of Judah. A century and a half before, the Prophet Jeremiah had given this word from the Lord: "For who will have pity on you, O Jerusalem? Or who will bemoan you? Or who will turn aside to ask how you are doing?" (Jer. 15:5, NKJV) *Nehemiah was the man God had chosen to do those very things!*

Some people prefer *not* to know what's going on, because information might bring obligation. "What you don't know can't hurt you," says the old adage; but is it true? In a letter to a Mrs. Foote, Mark Twain wrote, "All you need in this life is ignorance and confidence; then success is sure." But what we don't know *could* hurt us a great deal! There are people in the cemetery who chose not to know the truth. The slogan for the 1987 AIDS publicity campaign was "Don't die of ignorance"; and that slogan can be applied to many areas of life besides health.

Nehemiah asked about Jerusalem and the Jews living there because he had a caring heart. When we truly care about people, we want the facts, no matter how painful they may be. "Practical politics consists in ignoring facts," American historian Henry Adams said; but Aldous Huxley said, "Facts do not cease to exist because they are ignored." Closing our eyes and ears to the truth could be the first step toward tragedy for ourselves as well as for others.

What did Nehemiah learn about Jerusalem and the Jews? Three words summarize the bad news: remnant, ruin, and reproach. Instead of a land inhabited by a great nation, only a remnant of people lived there; and they were in great affliction and struggling to survive. Instead of a magnificent city, Jerusalem was in shambles; and where there had once been great glory, there was now nothing but great reproach.

Of course, Nehemiah had known all his life that the city of his fathers was in ruins, because the Babylonians had destroyed Jerusalem's walls, gates, and temple in 586 B.C. (2 Kings 25:1-21). Fifty years later, a group of 50,000 Jews had returned to Jerusalem to rebuild the temple and the city. Since the Gentiles had hindered their work, however, the temple was not completed for twenty years (Ezra 1–6), and the gates and walls never were repaired. Perhaps Nehemiah had hoped that the work on the walls had begun again and that the city was now restored. Without walls and gates, the city was open to ridicule and attack. See Psalms 48, 79, 84, and 87 to see how much loyal Jews loved their city.

Are we like Nehemiah, anxious to know the truth even about the worst situations? Is our interest born of concern or idle curiosity? When we read missionary prayer letters, the news in religious periodicals, or even our church's ministry reports, do we want the facts, and do the facts burden us? Are we the kind of people who care enough to ask?

2. He cared enough to weep (Neh. 1:4)

What makes people laugh or weep is often an indication of character. People who laugh at others' mistakes or misfortunes, or who weep over trivial personal disappointments, are lacking either in culture or character, and possibly both. Sometimes weeping is a sign of weakness; but with Nehemiah, it was a sign of strength, as it was with Jeremiah (Jer. 9:1), Paul (Acts 20:19), and the Lord Jesus (Luke 19:41). In fact, Nehemiah was like the Lord Jesus in that he willingly shared the burden that was crushing others. "The reproaches of them that reproached Thee are fallen upon Me" (Ps. 69:9; Rom. 15:3).

When God puts a burden on your heart, don't try to escape it; for if you do, you may miss the blessing He has planned for you. The Book of Nehemiah begins with "great affliction" (Neh. 1:3), but before it closes, there is great joy (8:12, 17). "Weeping may endure for a night, but joy cometh in the morning" (Ps. 30:5). Our tears water the "seeds of providence" that God has planted on our path; and without our tears, those seeds could never grow and produce fruit.

It was customary for the Jews to sit down when they mourned (Ezra 9:1-4; 2:13). Unconsciously, Nehemiah was imitating the grieving Jewish captives who had been exiled in Babylon years before (Ps. 137:1). Like Daniel, Nehemiah probably had a private room where he prayed to God with his face toward Jerusalem (Dan. 6:10; 1 Kings 8:28-30). Fasting was required of the Jews only once a year, on the annual Day of Atonement (Lev. 16:29); but Nehemiah spent several days fasting, weeping, and praying. He knew that somebody had to do something to rescue Jerusalem, and he was willing to go.

3. He cared enough to pray (Neh. 1:5-10)

This prayer is the first of twelve instances of prayer recorded in this book. (See 2:4; 4:4, 9; 5:19; 6:9, 14; 9:5ff; 13:14, 22, 29, 31.) The Book of Nehemiah opens and closes with prayer. It is obvious that Nehemiah was a man of faith who depended wholly on the Lord to help him accomplish the work He had called him to do. The Scottish novelist George MacDonald said, "In whatever man does without God, he must fail miserably, or succeed more miserably." Nehemiah succeeded because he depended on God. Speaking about the church's ministry today, the late Alan Redpath said, "There is too much working before men and too little waiting before God."

This prayer begins with *ascription of praise to God (1:5)*. "God of heaven" is the title Cyrus used for the Lord when he announced that the Jews could return to their land (2 Chron. 36:22-23; Ezra 1:1-2). The heathen gods were but idols on the earth, but the God of the Jews was Lord in heaven. Ezra often used this divine title (5:11-12; 6:9; 7:12, 21, 23), and it is found four times in Nehemiah (1:4-5; 2:4, 20) and three times in Daniel (2:18-19, 44). Nehemiah began his prayer as we should begin our prayers: "Our Father which art in heaven, Hallowed be Thy name" (Matt. 6:9).

To what kind of a God do we pray when we lift our prayers to "the God of heaven"? We pray to a "great and awesome God" (Neh. 1:5, NKJV; and see 4:14, 8:6, and 9:32), who is worthy of our praise and worship. If you are experiencing great affliction (v. 3) and are about to undertake a great work (4:19; 6:3), then you need the great power (1:10), great goodness (9:25, 35), and great mercy (v. 31) of a great God. Is the God you worship big enough to handle the challenges that you face?

He is also a God who keeps His Word (1:5). The Lord had made a covenant with His people Israel, promising to bless them richly if they obeyed His Word, but warning that He would chasten them if they disobeyed (Lev. 26; Deut. 27–30). The city of Jerusalem was in ruins, and the nation was feeble because the people had sinned against the Lord. (See Ezra's prayer of confession in Ezra 9 and the prayer of the nation in Neh. 9.)

The greater part of Nehemiah's prayer was devoted to *con-*

fession of sin (1:6-9). The God who promised blessing and chastening also promised forgiveness if His people would repent and turn back to Him (Deut. 30; 1 Kings 8:31-53). It was this promise that Nehemiah was claiming as he prayed for himself and the nation. God's eyes are upon His people and His ears are open to their prayers (1 Kings 8:29; 2 Chron. 7:14). The word *remember* is a key word in this book (Neh. 1:8; 4:14; 5:19; 6:14; 13:14, 22, 29, 31).

Note that Nehemiah used the pronoun "we" and not "they," identifying himself with the sins of a generation he didn't even know. It would have been easy to look back and blame his ancestors for the reproach of Jerusalem, but Nehemiah looked within and blamed himself! "We have sinned! We have dealt very corruptly!"

A few years ago, when the "media scandals" brought great reproach to the church, I wrote in my book *The Integrity Crisis:*

> To begin with, the integrity crisis involves more than a few people who were accused of moral and financial improprieties. *The integrity crisis involves the whole church.* I am not saying that people didn't sin, nor am I preaching "collective guilt," whatever that is. I only want to emphasize that, in the body of Christ, we belong to one another, we affect one another, and we can't escape one another. The press did not create the crisis, the church did; and the church will have to solve it (Nashville: Oliver-Nelson, 1988; p. 18).

When one Jewish soldier, Achan, sinned at Jericho, God said that "the children of Israel committed a trespass" and that "Israel" sinned and transgressed the covenant (Josh. 7:1, 11). Since the sin of one man was the sin of the whole nation, it brought shame and defeat to the whole nation. Once that sin had been dealt with, God could again bless His people with victory.

How do we know that God forgives our sins when we repent and confess to Him? *He has so promised in His Word.* Nehemiah's prayer is saturated with quotations from and allusions to the covenants of God found in Leviticus and Deuteronomy. He certainly knew the Old Testament Law! In Nehemiah 1:8-9, he reminded God of His words found in Deuteronomy 28:63-67 and 30:1-10, just as we remind the Lord of His promise in 1 John 1:9. Nehemiah asked God to forgive His people, regather them to their land, and restore them to His favor and blessing.

This humble prayer closed with *an expression of confidence (Neh. 1:10-11).* To begin with, he had confidence in the power of God. When the Bible speaks of the eyes, ears, and hands of the Lord, it is using only human language to describe divine activity. God is spirit, and therefore does not have a body such as humans have; but He is able to see His people's needs, hear their prayers, and work on their behalf with His mighty hand. Nehemiah knew that he was too weak to rebuild Jerusalem, but he had faith that God would work on his behalf.

He also had confidence in God's faithfulness. "Now these are Thy servants and Thy people" (v. 10). In bringing Babylon to destroy Jerusalem and take the people captive, God chastened the Jews sorely; but He did not forsake them! They were still His people and His servants. He had redeemed them from Egypt by His great power (Ex. 14:13-31) and had also set them free from bondage in Babylon. Would He not, in His faithfulness, help them rebuild the city?

Unlike Elijah, who thought he was the only faithful Jew left (1 Kings 19:10), Nehemiah had confidence that God would raise up other people to help him in his work. He was sure that many other Jews were also praying and that they would rally to the cause once they heard that God was at work. Great leaders are not only believing people who obey the Lord and courageously move ahead, but they also challenge others to go with them. You can't be a true leader unless you have followers, and Nehemiah was able to enlist others to help him do the work.

Finally, Nehemiah was confident that God would work in the heart of Artaxerxes and secure for the project the official support that it needed (Neh. 1:10). Nehemiah couldn't simply quit his job and move to Jerusalem. He was an appointee of the king, and he needed the king's permission for everything he did. Furthermore, he needed the king's provision and protection so he could travel to Jerusalem and remain away from his post until the work was completed. Without official authority to govern, an official guard for the journey, and the right to use materials from the king's forest, the entire project was destined to fail. Eastern monarchs were absolute despots, and it was not easy to approach them or convince them. But "the king's heart is in the hand of the Lord; He directs it like a watercourse wherever He pleases" (Prov. 21:2, NIV).

Too often, we plan our projects and then ask God to bless them; but Nehemiah didn't make that mistake. He sat down and wept (Neh. 1:4), knelt down and prayed, and then stood up and worked because he knew he had the blessing of the Lord on what he was doing.

4. He cared enough to volunteer (Neh. 1:11)

It has well been said that prayer is not getting man's will done in heaven but getting God's will done on earth. However, for God's will to be done on earth, He needs people to be available for Him to use. God does "exceedingly abundantly above all that we ask or think, according to the power that works *in us* (Eph. 3:20, NKJV, italics mine). If God is going to answer prayer, He must start by working in the one doing the praying! He works in us and through us to help us see our prayers answered.

While Nehemiah was praying, his burden for Jerusalem became greater and his vision of what needed to be done became clearer. Real prayer keeps your heart and your head in balance so your burden doesn't make you impatient to run ahead of the Lord and ruin everything. As we pray, God tells us *what* to do, *when* to do it, and *how* to do it; and all are important to the accomplishing of the will of God. Some Christian workers are like Lord Ronald in one of Stephen Leacock's short stories who "flung himself upon his horse and rode madly off in all directions."

Nehemiah planned to volunteer to go to Jerusalem to supervise the rebuilding of the walls. He didn't pray for God to send somebody else, nor did he argue that he was ill-equipped for such a difficult task. He simply said, "Here am I — send me!" He knew that he would have to approach the king and request a leave of absence. Eastern kings' word meant life or death. What would happen to Nehemiah's plans if he approached Artaxerxes on the wrong day, when the king was ill or displeased with something or someone in the palace? No matter how you look at it, Nehemiah was facing a test of faith; but he knew that his God was a great God and would see him through.

The king's cupbearer would have to sacrifice the comfort and security of the palace for the rigors and dangers of life in a ruined city. Luxury would be replaced by ruins, and prestige by ridicule and slander. Instead of sharing the king's bounties, Nehemiah would personally pay for the upkeep of scores of people who would eat at his table. He would leave behind the ease of the palace and take up the toils of encouraging a beaten people and finishing an almost impossible task.

And with the help of God, *he did it!* In fifty-two days, the walls were rebuilt, the gates were restored, and the people were rejoicing! And it all started with a man who cared.

Abraham cared and rescued Lot from Sodom (Gen. 18–19). Moses cared and delivered the Israelites from Egypt. David cared and brought the nation and the kingdom back to the Lord. Esther cared and risked her life to save her nation from genocide. Paul cared and took the Gospel throughout the Roman Empire. Jesus cared and died on the cross for a lost world.

God is still looking for people who care, people like Nehemiah, who cared enough to ask for the facts, weep over the needs, pray for God's help, and then volunteer to get the job done.

"Here am I, Lord—send me!"

The Mountain Starts to Move

Unknown to him, Nehemiah was about to join the glorious ranks of the "champions of faith"; and in the centuries to follow, his name would be included with heroes like Abraham, Joseph, Moses, Joshua, Esther, Deborah, and David. One person can make a big difference in this world, if that person knows God and really trusts in Him. Because faith makes a difference, we can make a difference in our world to the glory of God.

"Faith is a living, daring confidence in God's grace," said Martin Luther. "It is so sure and certain that a man could stake his life on it a thousand times." The promise is that "all things are possible to him who believes" (Mark 9:23, NKJV). Jesus said living faith can move mountains! (Matt. 17:20)

This chapter describes three evidences of Nehemiah's faith. As we study these evidences of faith, we must examine our own hearts to see whether or not we are really walking and working by faith.

1. He had the faith to wait (Neh. 2:1-3)

Since the Jewish month of Nisan would be our mid-March to mid-April, it would indicate that four months have passed since Nehemiah received the bad news about the plight of Jerusalem. As every believer should, Nehemiah patiently waited on the Lord for directions; because it is "through faith and patience" that we inherit the promises (Heb. 6:12). "He that believeth shall not make haste" (Isa. 28:16). True faith in God brings a calmness to the heart that keeps us from rushing about and trying to do in our own strength what only God can do. We must know not only how to *weep and pray,* but also how to *wait and pray.*

Three statements in Scripture have a calming effect on me whenever I get nervous and want to rush ahead of the Lord: "Stand still, and see the salvation of the Lord" (Ex. 14:13); "Sit still . . . until you know how the matter will turn out" (Ruth 3:18, NKJV); "Be still, and know that I am God" (Ps. 46:10). When you wait on the Lord in prayer, you are not wasting your time; you are investing it. God is preparing both you and your circumstances so that His purposes will be accomplished. However, when the right time arrives for us to act by faith, we dare not delay.

Eastern monarchs were sheltered from anything that might bring them unhappiness (Es. 4:1-2); but on that particular day, Nehemiah could not hide his sorrow. "By sorrow of the heart the spirit is broken" (Prov. 15:13), and Psalm 102 certainly describes Nehemiah's feelings about Jerusalem. Perhaps each morning, Nehemiah prayed, "Lord, if today is the day I speak to the king about our plans, then open the way for me."

The king noticed that his cupbearer was carrying a burden. Had Artaxerxes been in a bad mood, he might have banished Nehemiah or even ordered him killed; but instead, the king inquired why his servant was so sad. "The king's heart is in the hand of the Lord, as the rivers of water He turneth it whithersoever He will" (Prov. 21:1). World leaders are only God's servants, whether they know it or not. "O Lord God of our fathers, are You not the God who is in heaven? You rule over all the kingdoms of the nations. Power and might are in Your hand, and no one can withstand You" (2 Chron. 20:6, NIV).

2. He had the faith to ask (Neh. 2:4-8)

The king asked him, "What is it you want?" What an opportunity for Nehemiah! All the power and wealth of the kingdom were wrapped up in that question!

As he was accustomed to do, Nehemiah sent one of his quick "telegraph prayers" to the Lord (4:4; 5:9; 6:9, 14; 13:14, 22, 29, 31). But keep in mind that these "emergency prayers" were backed up by four months of fasting and praying. If Nehemiah had not been diligent to pray in private, his "telegraph prayers" might have gone unanswered. "He had only an instant for that prayer," wrote George Morrison. "Silence would have been misinterpreted. Had he closed his eyes and lingered in devotion, the king immediately would have suspected treason."[1]

It encourages my prayer life when I contrast the earthly throne of Artaxerxes with the throne of grace in heaven. Nehemiah had to wait for an invitation before he could share his burden with the king, but we can come to the throne of grace at any time with any need (Heb. 4:14-16). Artaxerxes saw the sorrow on Nehemiah's face, but our Lord sees our hearts and not only knows our sorrows but also feels them with us. People approaching the throne of Persia had to be very careful what they said, lest they anger the king; but God's people can tell Him whatever burdens them. (The word *boldly* in Heb. 4:16 means "freedom of speech.") You are never sure of the mood of a human leader, but you can always be sure of God's loving welcome.

---

1. Morrison, George. *Morning Sermons* (London: Hodder and Stoughton, 1935), p. 243

Jewish rabbis often answer a question with a question, and Nehemiah followed that example. Instead of telling the king what he planned to do, he aroused the king's sympathy and interest with a question regarding how he should feel about the sad plight of his ancestral city and the graves of his forefathers. It was good psychology, and God used Nehemiah's reply to get the king's sympathetic attention (Luke 21:14-15). A pagan monarch would probably not sorrow over the ruins of Jerusalem, but he would certainly show respect for the dead.

Nehemiah was a true patriot whose dreams for the future were motivated by the values of the past. He did not try to duplicate the past, for that was impossible; rather, he built on the past so that Israel would have a future. To Nehemiah, the past was a rudder to guide him and not an anchor to hold him back. When Samuel Johnson called patriotism "the last refuge of a scoundrel," he was referring to that temporary zeal that uses "love of country" as propaganda for selfish purposes. United States Ambassador to the United Nations Adlai Stevenson said that patriotism was not "a short and frenzied outburst of emotion, but the tranquil and steady dedication of a lifetime." That certainly describes Nehemiah's kind of patriotism.

Not only had Nehemiah *prayed* for this opportunity, but he had also *planned* for it and had his answer ready. During those four months of waiting, he had thought the matter through and knew exactly how he would approach the project. His reply to the king can be summarized in two requests: "Send me!" (Neh. 2:4-6) and "Give me!" (vv. 7-10)

Nehemiah could not leave his post without the approval of the king, nor could he work in Jerusalem without the authority of the king. Pressure from local officials had stopped the work once before (Ezra 4), and Nehemiah didn't want history to repeat itself. He asked Artaxerxes to appoint him governor of Judah and to give him the authority he needed to rebuild the city walls. He told the king when he expected to return, but we don't know what that date was. According to Nehemiah 5:14, Nehemiah spent twelve years as governor. He went back to Persia briefly to report to the king, but then returned to Jerusalem to correct the abuses that appeared during his absence (13:6-7).

But Nehemiah asked for even more. He needed letters of introduction that would guarantee safe travel and hospitality between Susa and Jerusalem. He also requested letters of authority that would provide the materials needed for the construction of buildings and walls. (Nehemiah had done his research well. He even knew the name of the keeper of the king's forest!) Artaxerxes gave him what he asked, but it was the good hand of God that made the king so cooperative (see 2:18; and Ezra 7:6, 9, 28).

When Jesus sent His disciples out to minister, He first gave them the authority they needed to do the job; and He promised to meet their every need (Matt. 10:1-15). As we go forth to serve the Lord, we have behind us all authority in heaven and on earth (28:18); so we don't have to be afraid. The important thing is that we go where He sends us and that we do the work He has called us to do.

Nehemiah is a good example of how believers should relate to unsaved officials as they seek to do the work of God. Nehemiah respected the king and sought to work within the lines of authority that existed in the empire. He didn't say, "I have a commission from the Lord to go to Jerusalem, and I'm going whether you like it or not!" When it comes to matters of conscience, we must always obey God rather than men (Acts 5:29); but even then, we must show respect for authority (see Rom. 13 and 1 Peter 2:11-25). Daniel and his friends took the same approach as did Nehemiah, and God honored them as well (Dan. 1).

The king's response is evidence of the sovereignty of God in the affairs of nations. We expect God to be able to work through a dedicated believer like Nehemiah, but we forget that God can also work through unbelievers to accomplish His will. He used Pharaoh to display His power in Egypt (Ex. 9:16; Rom. 9:17) and Cyrus to deliver His people from Babylon (Isa. 44:28; 45:1; Ezra 1:1-2). Caesar issued the decree that brought Mary and Joseph to Bethlehem (Luke 2:1-7), and two different Roman centurions — Claudius Lysias and Julius — saved Paul's life (Acts 21:26-40; 23:25-30; 27:1, 42-44). While it may be helpful to have believing officials like Joseph, Daniel, and Nehemiah, we must remember that God is not required to use only believers.

Moses and Nehemiah made similar decisions of faith and similar sacrifices (Heb. 11:24-26). As the representative of the deliverer of the Jews, would he be welcomed by the Gentile officials? Nehemiah performed no signs or wonders, nor did he deliver any prophecies; but he faithfully did his work and prepared a city for the coming Messiah (Dan. 9:24-27).

3. He had the faith to challenge others (Neh. 2:11-18a)
Traveling (Neh. 2:9-10). No description is given of the trip from Susa to Jerusalem, a journey of at least two months' time. As a testimony to the faithfulness of God, Ezra had refused military protection for his journey (Ezra 8:21-23); but since Nehemiah was a governor on official business, he had a military escort. Nehemiah had just as much faith as Ezra; but as the king's officer, he could not travel without his retinue. For one thing, he would not oppose the will of the king; and he could not force his faith upon others.

When the official caravan arrived, it was bound to attract attention, particularly among those who hated the Jews and wanted to keep them from fortifying their city. Three special enemies are named: Sanballat, from Beth Horan, about twelve miles from Jerusalem; Tobiah, an Ammonite; and Geshem, an Arabian (Neh. 2:19), also called "Gashmu" (6:6). Sanballat was Nehemiah's chief enemy, and the fact that he had some kind of official position in Samaria only made him that much more dangerous (4:1-3).

Being an Ammonite, Tobiah was an avowed enemy of the Jews (Deut. 23:3-4). He was related by marriage to some of Nehemiah's co-laborers and had many friends among the Jews (Neh. 6:17-19). In fact, he was "near of kin" ("allied") to Eliashib the priest (13:4-7). If Sanballat was in charge of the army, then Tobiah was director of the intelligence division of their operation. It was he who gathered "inside information" from his Jewish friends and passed it along to Sanballat and Geshem. Nehemiah would soon discover that his biggest problem was not the enemy on the outside but the compromisers on the inside, a problem the church still faces today.

Investigating (Neh. 2:11-16). After his long difficult journey, Nehemiah took time to rest; for leaders must take care of themselves if they are going to be able to serve the Lord (Mark 6:31). He also took time to get "the lay of the land" without arousing the concern of the enemy. A good leader doesn't rush into his work but patiently gathers the facts firsthand and then plans his strategy (Prov. 18:13). We must be "wise as serpents" because the enemy is always watching and waiting to attack.

Leaders are often awake when others are asleep, and working when others are resting. Nehemiah didn't want the enemy to know what he was doing, so he investigated the ruins by night. By keeping his counsel to himself, Nehemiah prevented Tobiah's friends from getting information they could pass along to Sanballat. A wise leader knows when to plan, when to speak, and when to work.

As he surveyed the situation, he moved from west to south to east, concentrating on the southern section of the city. It was just as his brother had reported: The walls were broken down and the gates were burned (Neh. 2:13; 1:3). Leaders must not live in a dream world. They must face facts honestly and accept the bad news as well as the good news. Nehemiah saw more at night than the residents saw in the daylight, for he saw the potential as well as the problems. That's what makes a leader!

Challenging (Neh. 2:17-20). Nehemiah's appeal was positive; he focused on the glory and greatness of the Lord. He had been in the city only a few days, but he spoke of "we" and "us" and not "you" and "them." As he did in his prayer (1:6-7), he identified with the people and their needs. The city was a reproach to the Lord (1:3; 4:4; 5:9), but the hand of the Lord was with them; and He would enable them to do the work. God had already proved His power by working in the heart of the king, and the king had promised to meet the needs. It was Nehemiah's personal burden for Jerusalem and his experience with the Lord that convinced the Jews that the time was right to build.

It is to the credit of the Jewish nobles that they accepted the challenge immediately and said, "Let us rise up and build!" They were not so accustomed to their situation that they took it for granted and decided that nothing could be changed. Nor did they remind Nehemiah that the Jews had once tried to repair the walls and were stopped (Ezra 4). "We tried that once and it didn't work. Why try again?"

Christian leaders today face these same two obstacles as they seek to lead God's people into new conquests for the Lord. How often we hear, "We're content the way things are; don't rock the boat by trying to change things." Or, "We tried that before and it didn't work!"

It is worth noting that God sent the Jews a *leader from the outside*. Nehemiah came into the community with a new perspective on the problems and a new vision for the work. Too often in a local church, new members have a hard time "breaking into the system" because the veterans are afraid of new ideas that might lead to change. Since most of their leadership comes up through the ranks, parachurch ministries must also beware of the "closed corporation" attitude. New workers from outside the organization might open the windows and let in some fresh air.

The good hand of God was upon the leader, and the followers "strengthened their hands" for the work (Neh. 2:8, 18). It takes both the hands of leadership and the hands of partnership to accomplish the work of the Lord. Leaders can't do the job by themselves, and workers can't accomplish much without leadership. Vincent de Paul said, "If in order to succeed in an enterprise, I were obliged to choose between fifty deer commanded by a lion, and fifty lions commanded by a deer, I should consider myself more certain of success with the first group than with the second."

Someone has defined *leadership* as "the art of getting people to do what they ought to do because they want to do it." If that definition is true, then Nehemiah certainly was a leader! Most of the people united behind him and risked their lives to get the work done.

Nehemiah was not only able to challenge his own people, but he was also able to stand up against the enemy and deal effectively with their opposition. Just as soon as God's people step out by faith to do His will, the enemy shows up and tries to discourage them. Sanballat and Tobiah heard about the enterprise (v. 10) and enlisted Geshem to join them in opposting the Jews. In chapters 4–7, Nehemiah will describe the different weapons the enemy used and how the Lord enabled him to defeat them.

They started off with ridicule, a device somebody has

called "the weapon of those who have no other." They laughed at the Jews and belittled both their resources and their plans. They even suggested that the Jews were rebelling against the king. That weapon had worked once before (see Ezra 4).

Whether in the area of science, exploration, invention, business, government, or Christian ministry, just about everyone who has ever accomplished anything has faced ridicule. Our Lord was ridiculed during His life and mocked while He was hanging on the cross. He was "despised and rejected of men" (Isa. 53:3). On the Day of Pentecost, some of the Jews in the crowd said that the Christians were drunk (Acts 2:13). The Greek philosophers called Paul a "babbler" (17:18, NIV), and Festus told Paul he was out of his mind (26:24).

Nehemiah could have dealt with their ridicule in several ways. He might have ignored it, and sometimes that's the wisest thing to do (Prov. 26:4). But at the beginning of an enterprise, it's important that leaders encourage their people and let them know that God has everything in control. Had Nehemiah ignored these three men who were important in the community, he might have weakened his own position among the Jews. After all, he was the official governor, and he was doing official business.

Or, Nehemiah might have debated with the three enemy leaders and tried to convince them that their position was false. But that approach would only have given "official promotion" to the three men along with opportunity for them to say more. Why should Nehemiah give the enemy opportunity to make speeches against the God whom he served?

Of course, Nehemiah would not ask them to join the project and work with the Jews, although Sanballat and his friends would have welcomed the invitation (Neh. 6:1-4). In his reply, Nehemiah made three things clear: Rebuilding the wall was God's work; the Jews were God's servants; and Sanballat, Tobiah, and Geshem had no part in the matter. Sometimes leaders have to negotiate, but there are times when leaders must draw a line and defend it. Unfortunately, not everybody in Jerusalem agreed with their leader; for some of them cooperated with Sanballat, Tobiah, and Geshem and added to Nehemiah's burdens.

The stage is now set and the drama is about to begin.

But before we join the workers on the wall, let's ask ourselves whether we are the kind of leaders and followers God wants us to be. Like Nehemiah, do we have a burden in our hearts for the work God has called us to do? (2:12) Are we willing to sacrifice to see His will accomplished? Are we patient in gathering facts and in planning our work? Do we enlist the help of others or try to do everything ourselves? Do we motivate people on the basis of the spiritual—what God is doing—or simply on the basis of the personal? Are they following us or the Lord as He leads us?

As followers, do we listen to what our leaders say as they share their burdens? Do we cling to the past or desire to see God do something new? Do we put our hands and necks to the work? (v. 18; 3:5) Are we cooperating in any way with the enemy and thus weakening the work? Have we found the job God wants us to complete?

Anyone can go through life as a destroyer; God has called His people to be builders. What an example Nehemiah is to us! Trace his "so" statements and see how God used him: "So I prayed" (2:4); "So I came to Jerusalem" (v. 11); "So they strengthened their hands for this good work" (v. 18); "So built we the wall" (4:6); "So we labored in the work" (v. 21); "So the wall was finished" (6:15).

Were it not for the dedication and determination that came from his faith in a great God, Nehemiah would never have accepted the challenge or finished the work. He had never seen the verse, but what Paul wrote in 1 Corinthians 15:58 was what kept him going: "Therefore, my beloved brethren, be steadfast, immovable, always abounding in the work of the Lord, knowing that your labor is not in vain in the Lord" (NKJV).

No matter how difficult the task, or how strong the opposition, BE DETERMINED! As Dr. V. Raymond Edman used to say, "It is always too soon to quit."

THREE

Wall to Wall Workers

Nehemiah faced a great challenge and had great faith in a great God, but he would have accomplished very little had there not been great dedication on the part of the people who helped him rebuild the wall. With the kind of humility that befits a godly leader, Nehemiah gave all the credit to the people when he wrote, "So built we the wall . . . for the people had a mind to work" (Neh. 4:6).

British humorist Jerome K. Jerome said, "I like work, it fascinates me. I can sit and look at it for hours." When it comes to the work of the Lord, there is no place for spectators or self-appointed advisors and critics; but there is always room for workers. As you study this chapter, you will discover principles that apply to all human labor, especially the work of building the church.

1. The purpose of the work

Nehemiah was concerned about only one thing, the glory of God. "Let us build up the wall of Jerusalem, that we be no more a reproach" (2:17; and see 1:3; 4:4; 5:9). The Gentiles delighted in mocking their Jewish neighbors by pointing out the dilapidated condition of Jerusalem. After all, the Jews claimed that their capital city was "beautiful for situation, the joy of the whole earth" (Ps. 48:2). They said that God loved "the gates of Zion more than all the dwellings of Jacob" (87:2). If God loved Jerusalem so much, why were the walls in ruin and the gates burned? Why was the "holy city" a reproach? Why didn't the Jews do something?

For the most part, the world today ignores the church. If it does pay any attention to the church, it is usually to condemn or mock. "If you are the people of God," unbelievers ask, "why are there so many scandals in the church? If God is so powerful, why is the church so weak?" Whether Christians like it or not, we are living in a day of reproach when "the glory has departed" (1 Sam. 4:21).

The purpose of all ministry is the glory of God and not the aggrandizement of religious leaders or organizations (1 Cor. 10:31; 2 Cor. 4:5). The words of Jesus in His high priestly prayer ought to be the motivating force in all Christian ministry: "I have glorified Thee on the earth; I have finished the work which Thou gavest Me to do" (John 17:4). God has a special task for each of His children (Eph. 2:10); and in the humble, faithful doing of that task, we glorify His name.

Of course, the rebuilding of the walls and the setting of the gates also meant protection and security for the people. Jerusalem was surrounded by enemies, and it seemed foolish for the residents to improve their property when nothing was safe from invasion and plunder. Over the years, the citizens had become accustomed to their plight. Like too many believers in the church today, they were content to live with the status quo. Then Nehemiah arrived on the scene and challenged them to rebuild the city to the glory of God.

2. The pattern of the work
Nehemiah was a leader who planned his work and worked his plan, and the way he did it is an example for us to follow.

Thirty-eight individual workers are named in this chapter, and forty-two different groups are identified. There were also many workers whom Nehemiah did not name whose labors were important; and each worker—named and anonymous—was assigned a place and a task.

"A great many people have got a false idea about the church," said evangelist D.L. Moody. "They have got an idea that the church is a place to rest in . . . to get into a nicely cushioned pew, and contribute to the charities, listen to the minister, and do their share to keep the church out of bankruptcy, is all they want. The idea of work for them—actual work in the church—never enters their minds."

In 1 Corinthians 12 and 14, Paul compared individual Christians to members of the human body: Each member is important, and each has a special function to perform. I recall the relief that came to my own heart when I realized that God didn't expect me to do everything in the church, but rather to use the gifts He gave me in the tasks that He assigned. When I started doing that, I discovered I was helping others discover and develop their own gifts; and all of us accomplished more for the Lord.

The people finished this difficult task because they obeyed the same leader, kept their eyes on the same goal, and worked together for the glory of God. Neither the enemy outside the city nor the difficulties inside the city distracted them from their God-given task. Like Paul, they said, "This one thing I do" (Phil. 3:13).

The word *built* is used six times in Nehemiah 3 and means "rebuilt." George Morrison reminds us "that for this restoration no *new* material was needed. In the debris of the ruined masonry lay all the material required . . . and it seems to me that is always so when the walls of Zion are rebuilt" *(Morning Sermons,* London: Hodder and Stoughton, 1931, p. 249). It is not by inventing clever new things that we take away the church's reproach, but by going back to the old truths that made the church great in ages past. They lie like stones in the dust, waiting for some burdened Nehemiah to recover them and use them.

The word *repair* is used thirty-five times; it means "to make strong and firm." Nehemiah wasn't interested in a "quick fix," a whitewashed wall that would soon crumble (Ezek. 13:1-16; 22:28). They were building to the glory of God, and therefore they did their best.

The gates of Jerusalem had been destroyed by fire (Neh. 1:3; Jer. 17:27; Lam. 1:4), so Nehemiah requisitioned timber from the king's forest and had new gates constructed (Neh. 2:8) and put into place (6:1; 7:1). The gates were important to the safety of the people and the control of who went in and out of the city (7:3; 13:15-22). If the Lord loves the gates of Zion (Ps. 87:2), then His people ought to love them too.

Locks and bars are mentioned five times (Neh. 3:3, 6, 13-15). *Locks* refer to the sockets into which the bars were fitted, thus making it difficult for anyone outside to open the gates. It isn't enough that we simply do the work of God; we must also make sure that what we do is protected from the enemy. "Watch out that you do not lose what you have worked for, but that you may be rewarded fully" (2 John 8, NIV).

3. The people in the work

As you get acquainted with the various people mentioned in Nehemiah 3, you will find yourself saying, "This is just like the church today!" Circumstances change but human nature remains pretty much the same.

God uses all kinds of people. The chapter mentions rulers and priests (vv. 1, 12-19), men and women (v. 12), professional craftsmen (vv. 8, 32), and even people from outside the city (vv. 2, 5, 7). There was a place for everyone, and a job for everyone to do.

WALL TO WALL WORKERS

Leaders must set the example (Neh. 3:1). If anybody in the city should have been busy in the work, it was the priests, for the glory of the Lord was involved in the project. That the high priest used his consecrated hands to do manual labor shows that he considered the work on the wall to be a ministry to the Lord. "Therefore, whether you eat or drink, or whatever you do, do all to the glory of God" (1 Cor. 10:31, NKJV). Eliashib enlisted the other priests to work at the sheep gate in the northeast corner of the city. Since the sacrifices came into the city that way, the priests would be especially interested in that part of the project.

Sad to say, Eliashib did not remain true to his calling; for later he allied with the enemy and created serious problems for Nehemiah (Neh. 13:4-9). Some people who enthusiastically begin their work may drop out or turn against it for one reason or another. Eliashib's grandson married a daughter of Sanballat (v. 28), and this alliance no doubt influenced the high priest.

Some people will not work (Neh. 3:5). Tekoa was a town about eleven miles from Jerusalem, and some of their people traveled to Jerusalem to assist in the work. What a contrast between these people and their nobles! The Tekoites built in *two* places on the wall (vv. 5 and 27), while their nobles refused to bend the neck and work in even *one* place. Were these "aristocrats" so important in their own eyes that they could not perform manual labor? Yet Paul was a tentmaker (Acts 18:3), and Jesus was a carpenter (Mark 6:3).

The Tekoites were not the only "outsiders" to go to Jerusalem to work on the wall; for men also came from Jericho (Neh. 3:2), Gibeon, and Mizpah (v. 7). Their loyalty to their nation and their Lord was greater than their local interests. They were certainly safer back in their own communities, but they risked their lives to do the work of the Lord (Acts 15:25-26).

Some people do more work than others (Neh. 3:11, 19, 21, 24, 27, 30). Most workers are glad to lay down their tools when their job is finished, but these people asked for additional assignments. It isn't enough for us to say that we have done as much as others; we must do as *much as we can* as long as the Lord enables us. Jesus asked, "What do you do more than others? (Matt. 5:47, NKJV)

Some do their work at home (Neh. 3:10, 23, 28-30). At least six different workers, plus an unknown number of priests, repaired the portions of the wall that were nearest to their own houses. If all of us would follow this example, our neighborhoods and cities would be in much better shape! Of course, there is a spiritual lesson here: Christian service begins at home. A Chinese proverb says, "Better to be kind at home than to burn incense in a far place"; and Paul wrote, "Let them learn first to shew piety at home" (1 Tim. 5:4).

Some people work harder than others (Neh. 3:20). Baruch is the only worker of whom it is said that the work was done "earnestly" ("zealously," NIV). The Hebrew word means "to burn or glow" and suggests that Baruch burned a lot of energy! "Whatever your hand finds to do, do it with all your might" (Ecc. 9:10, NIV). Paul admonished the slaves to work hard for their masters because they were really working for Christ (Eph. 6:5-8). Lazy workers not only rob themselves and the Lord, but they also rob their fellow workers. "He also that is slothful in his work is brother to him that is a great waster" (Prov. 18:9).

4. The places of the work
Nehemiah began his list of the "work stations" with the Sheep Gate in the northeast corner of the city (Neh. 3:1). Then he moved counterclockwise around the walls to the Gate Hammiphkad ("the Muster Gate"), which was adjacent to the Sheep Gate and just above the East Gate (v. 29). In his

record, he names ten gates and several towers and other land-marks. He describes the work on the north wall first (vv. 1-7), then the western wall (vv. 8-13), then the southern point of the city (v. 14), and finally the eastern wall (vv. 15-32).

His primary purpose was to document for posterity and the official records the names and accomplishments of the people who worked on the wall. Without straining the text, however, we can glean from this chapter some spiritual illustrations to encourage us in our own personal lives and ministries.

The Sheep Gate (Neh. 3:1, 32). This was the gate through which the animals were brought into the city, including the temple sacrifices. The gate was near the temple area, so it was logical that the priests make this their special project. This is the only gate of which it is recorded that it was "sanctified," that is, dedicated to God in a special way.

This gate reminds us of Jesus Christ, the Lamb of God who died for the sins of the world (John 1:29; 5:2). Nehemiah could have begun his record with any of the gates, but he chose to start and end the report with the Sheep Gate. Jesus is the "Alpha and Omega, the beginning and the ending" (Rev. 1:8). Apart from Him and His sacrifice, we would have nothing eternal and satisfying. Nothing is said about the gate's "locks and bars," for the way is never closed to the lost sinner who wants to come to the Savior.

The Fish Gate (Neh. 3:3). This was located to the west of the Sheep Gate, and between the two stood the Tower of Hammeah ("the hundred") and the Tower of Hananeel (v. 1). These two towers were a part of the city's defense system and were close to the citadel, where the soldiers guarded the temple and protected the northern approach to the city which was especially vulnerable. Merchants used this gate when they brought fish from the Mediterranean Sea, and there may have been a fish market near the gate. In any event, it was a key entrance to the city.

The Old Gate (Neh. 3:6) is probably the Corner Gate (2 Kings 14:13; Jer. 31:38), located at the northwest corner of the city. Some students identify this with the "Mishneh Gate"; the Hebrew word means "second quarter" or "new quarter" (Zeph. 1:10, NIV). In Nehemiah's day, the northwest section of the city was "the mishneh" or "new quarter"; and this gate led into it. What a paradox: the old gate leads into the new quarter! But it is from the old that we derive the new; and if we abandon the old, there can be nothing new (see Jer. 6:16 and Matt. 13:52).

The Valley Gate (Neh. 3:13) is where Nehemiah began his nocturnal investigation of the ruins of the city (2:13). It was located at the southwest corner of the city walls, about 500 yards from the Dung Gate; and both opened into the Valley of Hinnom. The workers here not only restored the gate, but they also repaired the section of the wall between the two gates. It is likely that this long section of the wall—over 1,700 feet—was not as severely damaged as the other sections.

Every Christian needs a "valley gate," for God opposes the proud but gives grace to the humble (1 Peter 5:5-6). It is only as we yield to Christ and serve others that we can truly enter into the fullness of the life He has for us (Phil. 2:1-11).

The Dung Gate (Neh. 3:14) was located at the southernmost tip of the city, near the Pool of Siloam. It was a main exit to the Valley of Hinnom, where the city disposed of its garbage. The word *gehenna* means "valley of Hinnom" and identified this area that Jesus used as a picture of hell, "where their worm dieth not, and their fire is not quenched" (Mark 9:44). King Manasseh had sacrificed children to idols in that valley (2 Chron. 33:6), and King Josiah had desecrated the place by turning it into a rubbish heap (2 Kings 23:10).

The sanitary disposal of waste materials is essential to the health of a city. This gate did not have a beautiful name, but it did perform an important service! It reminds us that, like the city, each of us individually must get rid of whatever defiles us, or it may destroy us (2 Cor. 7:1; 1 John 1:9).

The Fountain Gate (Neh. 3:15) was on the east wall, just north of the Dung Gate, in a very strategic location near the Pool of Siloam, the old City of David and the water tunnel built by King Hezekiah (2 Kings 20:20). The Gihon Spring that fed the water system was an important source of water in the city.

In the Bible, water for drinking is a picture of the Holy Spirit of God (John 7:37-39), while water for washing is a picture of the Word of God (Eph. 5:26; John 15:3). Spiritually speaking, we have moved from the Valley Gate (humility) to the Dung Gate (cleansing) to the Fountain Gate (fullness of the Spirit).

The Water Gate (Neh. 3:26) led from the old City of David to the Gihon Spring, located adjacent to the Kidron Valley. Jerusalem was one of the few great cities of antiquity that was not built near a great river, and the city depended on reservoirs and springs for its water. The text does not say that this gate was repaired, but only that the workers repaired the walls adjacent to it. The "Nethinims" ("those who are given") were probably temple servants, descendants of the Gibeonites who were made drawers of water (Josh. 9:23). They would naturally want to live near the most important source of water for the city.

If the Fountain Gate reminds us of the Spirit of God, the Water Gate reminds us of the Word of God. In fact, it was at the Water Gate that Ezra and the priests conducted a great "Bible conference" and explained the Scriptures to the people (8:1ff). That this gate is not said to have been repaired, as were the others, suggests that the Word of God stands forever and will not fail (Ps. 119:89; Matt. 24:35). The Bible does not need to be repaired or improved.

"The Ophel" (Neh. 3:26-27) was a hill south of the temple area, between the Horse Gate and the Water Gate. It was especially fortified and had a tower. The temple servants lived in that area because it was close to the water supply.

The Horse Gate (Neh. 3:28) stood north of the Water Gate, adjacent to the temple area. It was here that wicked Athaliah was executed (2 Chron. 23:15). God warned His people not to trust in horses and chariots (Deut. 17:14-20), but Solomon imported them from Egypt (1 Kings 10:26-29), and they became an important part of the nation's defense system (Isa. 2:7). The Horse Gate reminds us that there is warfare in the Christian life (2 Tim. 2:1-4) and that we must always be ready to do battle (Eph. 6:10-18). It is significant that the priests repaired this gate as well as the Sheep Gate. Both were near the temple area.

The East Gate (Neh. 3:29) led directly to the temple and is probably what we know today as the Golden Gate. Tradition says that Jesus entered the temple on Palm Sunday through this gate. In the sixteenth century, the gate was sealed up with blocks of stone by the Turkish sultan, Sulayman the Magnificent. Jewish and Christian tradition both connect the Golden Gate with the coming of the Messiah to Jerusalem, and Muslims associate it with the future judgment.

Ezekiel saw the glory of the Lord depart from the temple at the East Gate (Ezek. 10:16-22; 11:22-25), and the Lord will return to the city the same way (43:1-5). So, we have every reason to associate this gate with the coming of the Lord and to remind ourselves to "abide in Him; that, when He shall appear, we may have confidence, and not be ashamed before Him at His coming" (1 John 2:28).

The Gate Hammiphkad (Neh. 3:31) was located at the northeast corner of the city. The Hebrew word has a military connotation and refers to the mustering of the troops for numbering and inspection. The NIV and NASB both translate it "the Inspection Gate." This is where the army was reviewed and registered. The north side of Jerusalem was the most vulnerable to attack, so this was a logical place to locate the army. When our Lord returns, He will gather His people together and review their works in preparation for giving out rewards for faithful service (1 Cor. 3:10-15; 2 Cor. 5:9-10; Rom. 14:10-12).

In this report, Nehemiah does not mention the Gate of Ephraim (Neh. 8:16; 12:39) or the Gate of the Guard (12:39). The former may have been on the north wall, looking toward the area of Ephraim; and the latter may have been associated in some way with "The Inspection Gate." Some translate it "The Prison Gate." It may have been the "court of the guard" named in 3:25.

Nehemiah's record ends with the Sheep Gate (v. 32), the place where he began (v. 1). Because they have rejected their Messiah, the people of Israel today have no sacrifice, no temple, and no priesthood (Hosea 3:4). Thank the Lord, here and there, individual Jews are trusting Christ; but the nation as a whole is blinded in unbelief (Rom. 11:25ff). When they see their Messiah, they will believe and be saved (Zech. 12:10–13:1).

No one person could have accomplished the work of repairing the walls and restoring the gates. It took leadership on Nehemiah's part and cooperation on the part of the people. Each had a place to fill and a job to do. So it is with the church today: We must work together if we are to finish the work to the glory of God.

"Therefore, my beloved brethren, be steadfast, immovable, always abounding in the work of the Lord, knowing that your labor is not in vain in the Lord" (1 Cor. 15:58, NKJV).

Workers and Warriors

The Bible tells us to love our neighbors, and also to love our enemies; probably because they are generally the same people."

Those words from Gilbert Keith Chesterton were certainly true in Nehemiah's situation. His arrival in Jerusalem was a threat to Sanballat and his associates (2:10), who wanted to keep the Jews weak and dependent. A strong Jerusalem would endanger the balance of power in the region, and it would also rob Sanballat and his friends of influence and wealth.

When things are going well, get ready for trouble, because the enemy doesn't want to see the work of the Lord make progress. As long as the people in Jerusalem were content with their sad lot, the enemy left them alone; but, when the Jews began to serve the Lord and bring glory to God's name, the enemy became active.

Opposition is not only an evidence that God is blessing, but it is also an opportunity for us to grow. The difficulties that came to the work brought out the best in Nehemiah and his people. Satan wanted to use these problems as weapons to destroy the work, but God used them as tools to build His people. "God had one Son without sin," said Charles Spurgeon, "but He never had a son without trial."

When Sir James Thornhill was painting the inside of the cupola of St. Paul's Cathedral in London, at one point he finished an area and stepped back to view it. Had he gone back one step more, he would have fallen from the scaffolding and perhaps killed himself. Seeing the situation, a friend seized one of the brushes and rubbed paint over a part of the picture. The artist rushed forward to protect his work, and at the same time, his life was saved. When the picture of our life or ministry is not all we think it ought to be, perhaps the Master Artist is rescuing us from something far worse and preparing us for something far better.

Chapters 4 to 6 describe at least nine different tactics that the enemy used to try to stop the work on the walls. First, they attacked the Jewish people with *ridicule (4:1-6)* and *plots of war (vv. 7-9)*. This resulted in difficulties *within* the Jewish ranks: *discouragement (v. 10), fear (vv. 11-23),* and *selfishness (5:1-19)*. When attacks on the people failed to stop the work, the enemy then started to attack their leader, Nehemiah. They tried *compromise (6:1-4), slander (vv. 5-9), threats (vv. 10-14)* and *intrigue (vv. 17-19);* but none of these devices worked either. Nehemiah was "steadfast and unmovable" and led his people to finish the work in fifty-two days!

Referring to Satan, Paul wrote, "For we are not ignorant of his devices" (2 Cor. 2:11). This chapter presents four of Satan's devices for opposing the Lord's work, and it also tells us how God's people can be steadfast and defeat the enemy. If you start building, you will soon be battling; so, be prepared!

1. Ridicule (Neh. 4:1-6)

British critic and author Thomas Carlyle called ridicule "the language of the devil." Some people who can stand bravely when they are shot at will collapse when they are laughed at.

Shakespeare called ridicule "paper bullets of the brain," but those bullets have slain many a warrior.

It is not unusual for the enemy to insult the servants of God. Goliath ridiculed David when the shepherd boy met the giant with only a sling in his hand (1 Sam. 17:41-47). Jesus was mocked by the soldiers during His trial (Luke 22:63-65) and by the rabble while He was hanging on the cross (23:35-37); and some of the heroes of the faith had to endure mocking (Heb. 11:36). *When the enemy laughs at what God's people are doing, it is usually a sign that God is going to bless His people in a wonderful way.* When the enemy rages on earth, God laughs in heaven (Ps. 2:4).

Sanballat and his friends had begun to ridicule the Jews even before the work on the wall had begun. "They laughed us to scorn," wrote Nehemiah, "and despised us" (Neh. 2:19). What special relationship Sanballat had with the army of Samaria is not explained to us. Perhaps he had the army assembled as a show of strength to frighten the Jews. By making his initial speech before the army, Sanballat intensified the power of his ridicule as he made some important people laugh at the Jews.

First, Sanballat ridiculed *the workers* by calling them "feeble Jews" (4:2). The word *feeble* means "withered, miserable." The people were like cut flowers that were fading away. They had no human resources that people could see, but the enemy could not see their great spiritual resources. The people of the world don't understand that God delights in using feeble instruments to get His work accomplished (1 Cor. 1:18-31). The world glories in its wealth and power, but God's people glory in their poverty and weakness. When we are weak, then we are strong (2 Cor. 12:1-10).

Then Sanballat ridiculed *the work itself* by asking three taunting questions. "Will they fortify themselves?" must have evoked gales of laughter from the Samaritan army. How could a remnant of feeble Jews hope to build a wall strong enough to protect the city from the army? "Will they sacrifice?" implies, "It will take more than prayer and worship to rebuild the city!" This question was blasphemy against Jehovah God, for Sanballat was denying that God would help His people. "Will they finish in a day?" suggests that the Jews didn't know how difficult the task was and would soon call it quits.

In his final question, Sanballat ridiculed *the materials* they were using. The stones were taken out of the rubbish heaps and probably were so old and damaged that they would never last when set into the wall. While it is true that limestone is softened by fire, it is also true that the walls were "broken down," while the gates were "consumed with fire" (Neh. 2:13). In spite of what Sanballat said, there was still plenty of good material for the builders to use.

Tobiah the Ammonite was one of the visiting dignitaries at the Samaritan army inspection; and when it was his turn to make a speech, he ridiculed *the finished product (4:3)*. You wouldn't need an army to knock down the wall; a solitary fox could do it! Of course, much that Sanballat and Tobiah said was true *from a human point of view;* for the Jewish remnant was weak and poor, and the work was too great for them. But they had great faith in a great God, and that's what made the difference.

How did Nehemiah respond to this ridicule? *He prayed and asked God to fight the enemy for him.* This is the third time you find Nehemiah praying (1:4-11; 2:4), and it will not be the last time. Nehemiah didn't allow himself to get detoured from his work by taking time to reply to their words. The Lord had heard the sneering taunts of Sanballat and Tobiah, and He would deal with them in His own way and His own time.

Nehemiah's prayer resembles the "imprecatory psalms," such as Psalms 69; 79; and 139:19-22. We must remember that Nehemiah was praying as a servant of God concerned for the glory of God. He was not requesting personal vengeance but official vindication for God's people. The enemy had blasphemously provoked God before the builders, and this was a terrible sin. The opposition of Sanballat and Tobiah against the Jews was in reality opposition against God.

The things people say may *hurt* us, but they can never *harm* us, unless we let them get into our system and poison us. If we spend time pondering the enemy's words, we will give Satan a foothold from which he can launch another attack closer to home. The best thing to do is to pray and commit the whole thing to the Lord; and then *get back to your work!* Anything that keeps you from doing what God has called you to do will only help the enemy.

2. Intimidating plots (Neh. 4:7-9)

A common enemy and a common cause brought four different groups together to stop the work on the walls of Jerusalem. The city was now completely surrounded by enemies! To the north were Sanballat and the Samaritans; to the east, Tobiah and the Ammonites; to the south, Geshem and the Arabs; and to the west, the Ashdodites. Ashdod was perhaps the most important city in Philistia at that time, and the Philistines did not want to see a strong community in Jerusalem.

God's people sometimes have difficulty working together, but the people of the world have no problem uniting in opposition to the work of the Lord (Ps. 2:1-2; Acts 4:23-30; Luke 23:12). As the enemy saw the work progressing, they became angry and decided to plan a secret attack against Jerusalem. Satan hates the Jews and has used one nation after another to try to destroy them (see Ps. 85 and Rev. 12). God chose the Jews to be His vehicle for giving the world the knowledge of the true God, the Scriptures, and the Savior (Rom. 9:1-5). "Salvation is of the Jews" (John 4:22), and Satan wanted to prevent the Savior from coming into the world. If he could destroy the nation, he would frustrate God's plan.

Nehemiah suspected that his enemies would launch an attack, so he posted a guard and encouraged the people to pray. The workers held both tools and weapons (Neh. 4:17) and were prepared to fight when the signal was given. "Watch and pray" combines faith and works and is a good example for us to follow in our work and our warfare (see Mark 13:33; 14:38; Eph. 6:18; Col. 4:2-4).

The Christian's battle is not against flesh and blood, but against Satan and his demonic forces that use flesh and blood to oppose the Lord's work. If we hope to win the war and finish the work, we must use the spiritual equipment God has provided (Eph. 6:10-18; 2 Cor. 10:1-6). If we focus on the *visible* enemy alone and forget the *invisible* enemy, we are sure to start trusting our own resources; and this will lead to defeat.

3. Discouragement (Neh. 4:10)

Pressures from without often create problems from within. It isn't easy to carry on your work when you are surrounded by danger and daily face the demands of a task that seems impossible. If the Jews became discouraged, they would defeat themselves; and Sanballat and his allies would never have to wage war.

Discouragement is a key weapon in Satan's arsenal. It was discouragement that kept Israel from entering the Promised Land at Kadesh-Barnea (Num. 13). "We be not able to go up against the people; for they are stronger than we" (v. 31). The ten unbelieving spies "discouraged the heart of the children of Israel" (32:9); and as a result, the nation wandered in the wilderness forty years until the new generation was ready to conquer the land.

"We are not able!" is the rallying cry of all who take their eyes off the Lord and start looking at themselves and their problems. These discouraged Jewish workers were actually agreeing with the enemy who said they were feeble! (Neh. 2:19; 4:1-3) Sanballat had openly declared that the work would stop, and it almost did.

Why did this discouragement arise from the royal tribe of Judah? (See Gen. 49:8-12.) They had David's blood in their veins, and you would think they would be men and women of great faith and courage. The answer is found in Nehemiah 6:17-19: Some people in the tribe of Judah were secretly cooperating with the enemy. The ties of marriage were stronger than the bonds of commitment to the Lord. According to 13:15-22, some of the leaders of Judah were not wholly devoted to the Lord, but were more interested in making money. The combination of marriage and money divided their loyalties, and they became the cause of discouragement.

In over forty years of ministry, I have learned that, in the Lord's work, *discouragers are often doubters and compromisers.* There is usually something wrong in their spiritual walk. They frequently lack faith in God's Word, for one thing; and they are primarily interested in their own plans and pursuits. A double-minded person is unbelieving and unstable (James 1:5-8) and hinders the work of the Lord.

Nehemiah didn't pay much attention to these complainers but went right on with the work. That's the best thing to do. If you take time away from your work to listen to everybody who wants your attention, you will never get anything done. Nehemiah got his encouragement from prayer and the promises of God, and the occasional complaints of some of the people didn't upset him.

4. Fear (Neh. 4:11-23)

The Jews who lived in the outlying villages (3:2, 5, 7, 13) kept bringing a report to the city that the enemy was planning another surprise attack. Whether these Jews were merely spreading rumors or helping to promote a conspiracy, we don't know; but they told the story repeatedly. ("Ten times" is a Hebrew phrase meaning "many times." See Gen. 31:41 and Num. 14:22.) Nehemiah didn't respond immediately and probably was praying for God's guidance. He himself was not afraid of the enemy; but when he saw that his people were starting to become afraid, he began to act.

In his First Inaugural Address, on March 4, 1933, President Franklin Delano Roosevelt said to a nation in the grip of an economic depression, "The only thing we have to fear is fear itself." He may have borrowed the thought from Henry David Thoreau, American naturalist, who wrote in his journal on September 7, 1851, "Nothing is so much to be feared as fear." Why? Because fear paralyzes you, and fear is contagious and paralyzes others. Fear and faith cannot live together in the same heart. "Why are ye fearful, O ye of little faith?" (Matt. 8:26) Frightened people discourage others and help bring defeat (Deut. 20:8).

Nehemiah's first step was to post guards at the most conspicuous and vulnerable places on the wall. The enemy could then see that the Jews were prepared to fight. He armed entire families, knowing that they would stand together and encourage one another. The Jews not only repaired the walls near their own houses (Neh. 3:28-30), but they stood with their families to protect their homes and their city.

After looking the situation over, Nehemiah then encouraged the people not to be afraid but to look to the Lord for help. If we fear the Lord, we need not fear the enemy. Nehemiah's heart was captivated by the "great and terrible" God of Israel (4:14; see 1:5), and he knew that God was strong enough to meet the challenge. He also reminded the people that they were fighting for their nation, their city, and their families. If the nation was destroyed, what would become of

God's great promises to Israel and His plan of redemption?

When we face a situation that creates fear in our hearts, we must remind ourselves of the greatness of God. If we walk by sight and view God through the problems, we will fail, as did the Jews at Kadesh-Barnea (Num. 13:26-33). But if we look at the problem through the greatness of God, we will have confidence and succeed. That was the approach David took when he faced Goliath (1 Sam. 17:45-47).

When the enemy learned that Jerusalem was armed and ready, they backed off (Neh. 4:15). God had frustrated their plot. "The Lord brings the counsel of the nations to nothing; He makes the plans of the peoples of no effect. The counsel of the Lord stands forever, the plans of His heart to all generations" (Ps. 33:10-11, NKJV). It is good to remind ourselves that the will of God comes from the heart of God and that we need not be afraid.

Nehemiah knew that he couldn't interrupt the work every time he heard a new rumor, so he set up a defense plan that solved the problem: Half of the men worked on the wall while the other half stood guard. He saw to it that the people carrying materials also carried weapons and that the workers on the walls carried swords. In this way, the work would not be interrupted, and the workers would be ready in case of an alarm. The man with the trumpet stayed close to Nehemiah so the alarm could be given immediately. The people were prepared to fight (Neh. 4:14), but they realized that it was God who fought with them and He alone could give the victory.

When Charles Spurgeon started his church magazine in 1865, he borrowed the title from Nehemiah and called the publication *The Sword and Trowel.* He said it was "a record of combat with sin and labor for the Lord." It is not enough to build the wall; we must also be on guard lest the enemy take it from us. Building and battling are both a normal part of the

Christian life if we are faithful disciples (Luke 14:28-33).

Again, Nehemiah spoke words of encouragement to the people (Neh. 4:19-20). He reminded them that they were involved in a great work. After all, they were serving a great God and rebuilding the walls of a great city. He also reminded them that they were not working alone, even though they couldn't see all of their fellow workers on the wall. God was with all of them and would come to their defense.

No matter what the workers were doing, or where they labored on the wall, they all kept an ear open for the sound of the trumpet. What an example for us to follow as we await the return of the Lord! "For the Lord Himself shall descend from heaven with a shout, with the voice of the archangel, and with the trump of God" (1 Thes. 4:16).

Nehemiah also instituted a "second shift" and required the workers from the other towns to stay in Jerusalem at night and help guard the city. It is often while we sleep that the enemy does his most insidious work (Matt. 13:25), and we must be on guard.

Nehemiah not only organized the workers and guards and encouraged them to trust the Lord, but he also set the right kind of example before them (Neh. 4:23). He was a leader who served and a servant who led. He stayed on the job and was alert at all times. He inspected the city's defenses every night and made sure that the guards were on duty.

The late Dr. Alan Redpath explained why the Jews succeeded in getting their work done and keeping the enemy at bay: The people had a mind to work (v. 6), a heart to pray (v. 9), an eye to watch (v. 9), and an ear to hear (v. 20); and this gave them the victory (*Victorious Christian Service*, Revell, 1958; pp. 76–79).

They also had a godly leader with the faith to stand.

"Therefore . . . be steadfast, immovable, always abounding in the work of the Lord" (1 Cor. 15:58, NKJV).

Stop! Thief!

When the enemy fails in his attacks from the *outside,* he then begins to attack from *within;* and one of his favorite weapons is *selfishness.* If he can get us thinking only about ourselves and what we want, then he will win the victory before we realize that he is even at work.

Selfishness means putting myself at the center of everything and insisting on getting what I want when I want it. It means exploiting others so I can be happy and taking advantage of them just so I can have my own way. It is not only wanting my own way but expecting everybody else to want my way too. Why are selfish people so miserable? I think Thomas Merton said it best: "To consider persons and events and situations only in the light of their effect upon myself is to live on the doorstep of hell."

This chapter reveals to us the depths of sin in the human heart and how each of us must learn to love our neighbors as ourselves. This moving drama has three acts.

1. A great cry (Neh. 5:1-5)
In the midst of a "great work" (4:19) for a "great God" (1:5), a "great cry" (5:1) was heard among the Jews. They were not

crying out against the Samaritans, the Ammonites, or the Arabs, but against their own people! Jew was exploiting Jew, and the economic situation had become so desperate that even the wives (who usually kept silent) were joining in the protest.

Four different groups of people were involved in this crisis. First, there were the people who owned no land but who needed food (v. 2). The population was increasing; there was a famine (v. 3); and the people were hungry. These people could not help themselves so they cried out to Nehemiah for help.

The second group was composed of landowners who had mortgaged their property in order to buy food (v. 3). Apparently inflation was on the rise, and prices were going higher. The combination of debt and inflation is enough to wipe out a person's equity very quickly.

The third group complained because the taxes were too high, and they were forced to borrow money to pay them (v. 4). In order to borrow the money, they had to give security; and this meant eventually losing their property. The Persian king received a fortune in annual tribute, very little of which ever benefited the local provinces. Unlike our situation today, the taxes did not support local services; they only supported the king.

The fourth group was made up of wealthy Jews who were exploiting their own brothers and sisters by loaning them money and taking their lands and their children for collateral (Lev. 25:39-40). Jewish boys and girls had to choose between starvation or servitude!

It was not unlawful for Jews to loan money to one another, but they were not to act like money lenders and charge interest (Deut. 23:19-20). They were to treat one another with love even in the matter of taking security (24:10-13; Ex. 22:25-27) or making a brother a servant (Lev. 25:35-46). Both the people and the land belonged to the Lord, and He would not have anybody using either one for personal gain.

One reason for the "Year of Jubilee" (Lev. 25) was to balance the economic system in Israel so that the rich could not get richer as the poor became poorer. All debts had to be forgiven in the fiftieth year, all land restored to its original owners, and all servants set free.

These wealthy businessmen were selfishly exploiting the poor in order to make themselves rich. They were using their power to rob some and to put others into bondage. Greed was one of the sins the prophets had denounced before the Babylonian Captivity (Isa. 56:9-12; Jer. 22:13-19; Amos 2:6-7; 5:11-12). God has a special concern for the poor and will not hold those guiltless who take advantage of them.

2. A great assembly (Neh. 5:6-13)

It is one thing to confront foreign enemies and quite something else to deal with your own people when they fight one another. Young Moses learned that it was easier to dispose of an Egyptian master than to reconcile two Jewish brothers (Ex. 2:11-15). Nehemiah showed true leadership in his responses to the problem.

Anger (Neh. 5:6). This was not the flaring up of a sinful temper but the expression of righteous indignation at the way the businessmen were oppressing their brothers and sisters. "In your anger do not sin" (Eph. 4:26, NIV; see Ps. 4:4). Nehemiah was not a politician who asked, "What is popular?" or a diplomat who asked, "What is safe?" but a true leader who asked, "What is right?" His was a holy anger against sin, and he knew he had the Law of God behind him. Moses expressed this kind of holy anger when he broke the stone tables of Law (Ex. 32), and so did Jesus when He saw the hardening of the Pharisees' hearts (Mark 3:5).

Why didn't Nehemiah know about this scandalous economic problem sooner? Probably because he was so immersed in the one thing he came to do—the rebuilding of the walls—that he had no time to get involved in the internal affairs of the community. His commission as governor was to repair the walls and restore the gates, not to reform the community. Furthermore, Nehemiah had not been in the city long enough to learn all that was going on.

It is important to note that the building of the wall did not *create* these problems; it *revealed* them. Often when a church enters into a building program, all sorts of problems start to surface that people didn't even know were there. A building program is a demanding thing that tests our faith, our patience, and our priorities; and while it brings out the best in some people, it can often bring out the worst in others.

Consultation (Neh. 5:7). "I consulted with myself" means literally "My heart consulted within me." A friend of mine calls this "putting my heads together." Actually, Nehemiah put his heart and his head together as he pondered the problem and sought God's direction. He got control of his feelings and his thoughts so that he could give constructive leadership to the people. "He who is slow to anger is better than the mighty, and he who rules his spirit than he who takes a city" (Prov. 16:32, NKJV). If a leader can't control himself, he will never be successful in controlling others.

Nehemiah decided to call a great assembly (Neh. 5:7) and publicly confront the people whose selfishness had created this difficult and painful situation. Theirs was a grievous public sin, involving the whole nation; and it demanded public rebuke and repentance.

Rebuke (Neh. 5:7-11). Nehemiah's rebuke of the exploiters consisted of six different appeals. First, he appealed to *their love* by reminding them that they were robbing their own fellow Jews, not the Gentiles (v. 7). The word "brother" is used four times in this speech. "Behold, how good and how pleasant it is for brethren to dwell together in unity!" (Ps. 133:1) "Let's not have any quarreling between you and me," Abraham said to Lot, "for we are brothers" (Gen. 13:8, NIV).

His appeal was based solidly on *the Word of God,* for the Law of Moses forbade Jews to exact interest from one another. The Jewish nation went into Babylonian Captivity an agricultural people, but some of them came out a mercantile people, having learned how to use money to make money. There is certainly nothing wrong with lending money (Matt. 25:27), providing you don't violate God's Word and exploit those who are helpless.

It is remarkable how much the Bible has to say about the right and wrong use of money. It is also remarkable how many professed believers ignore these truths and use their resources without consulting the Lord. They think that because they tithe, or give offerings to the Lord, they can do what they please with the rest of their income. They forget that we are stewards of all that God gives us, not just of what we give Him; and that He will hold us accountable for our stewardship.

In his third appeal, Nehemiah reminded them of *God's redemptive purpose for Israel (Neh. 5:8).* In the past, God redeemed Israel from Egypt; and more recently, He had redeemed them from Captivity in Babylon. But this verse informs us that Nehemiah and others of the leading Jews had helped redeem some of their people, and now their fellow Jews were putting people into bondage just to make money. These selfish money lenders were tearing down everything that God and Nehemiah were trying to build up.

What is freedom? It is life governed by truth and motivated by love. But the Jewish brokers were motivated by greed and ignoring the truth of God's Word. Their selfishness put both themselves and their creditors into bondage.

Israel's witness to their Gentile neighbors (v. 9) was the

63

fourth appeal Nehemiah presented to the guilty money lenders. God called Israel to be a "light to the Gentiles" (Isa. 42:6; 49:6), but their conduct was certainly anything but a witness to their pagan neighbors. How could some of the Jewish citizens build the city wall on the one hand but enslave their neighbors on the other hand? If we truly fear the Lord, then we will want to honor Him before those who don't believe in Him.

Paul used a similar approach when he censured the Corinthian Christians for taking one another to court. "Dare any of you, having a matter against another, go to law before the unrighteous, and not before the saints? . . . But brother goes to law against brother, and that before unbelievers!" (1 Cor. 6:1, 6, NKJV) Far better to lose money than lose the privilege of your witness to the lost. You can always earn more money, but how do you restore a damaged testimony?

"The fear of our God" is not the servile dread of a slave toward a master but the loving respect of a child toward a parent. To fear the Lord means to seek to glorify God in everything we do. It means listening to His Word, honoring it, and obeying it. "The remarkable thing about fearing God," wrote Oswald Chambers, "is that when you fear God, you fear nothing else, whereas if you do not fear God, you fear everything else." Because Nehemiah's life was motivated by the fear of the Lord (Neh. 5:15), he did not fear what the enemy might do (vv. 14, 19). The fear of the Lord moved Nehemiah to be a faithful servant of the Lord.

To walk in the fear of God, of course, means to walk by faith, trusting God to deal with your enemies and one day balance the accounts. It means claiming Matthew 6:33 and having the right priorities in life. "The fear of the Lord leads to life, and he who has it will abide in satisfaction; he will not be visited with evil" (Prov. 19:23, NKJV).

In Nehemiah 5:10-11, Nehemiah appealed to *his own per-*

sonal practice. He was lending money to the needy, but he was not charging interest or robbing them of their security (Ex. 22:25). Unlike some leaders, Nehemiah was not saying, "Do what I say, not what I do!" He was not a hypocrite; he practiced what he preached. In fact, this chapter will conclude with Nehemiah pointing out all that God had enabled him to do for his people (Neh. 5:14-19). He was a good example as a believer and as a leader.

"The hundredth part" in verse 11 was the interest charged for the money, probably applied monthly, making a total of 12 percent interest a year. This practice had been going on before Nehemiah arrived on the scene and now the people were in despair as they tried to balance the family budget.

A man of action, Nehemiah told the brokers to restore both the interest and the security they had taken from their fellow Jews, as well as the property they had claimed in foreclosure. This drastic step of faith and love would not immediately solve all the economic problems of the people, but it would at least keep the problems from getting worse. It would also give the suffering people opportunity to make a fresh new start.

Nehemiah's sixth appeal was to remind them of *the judgment of the Lord (vv. 12-13).* The brokers promised to obey, so Nehemiah had them take an oath in the presence of the priests and the other officers of the city. This meant that their promise was not only between them and their neighbors, but between them and the Lord; and this was a serious thing. "When you make a vow to God, do not delay in fulfilling it. He has no pleasure in fools; fulfill your vow. It is better not to vow than to make a vow and not fulfill it" (Ecc. 5:4-5, NIV).

The great assembly was concluded with three actions that emphasized the seriousness of the occasion. First, Nehemiah shook out the folds of his robe, symbolic of what God would do with the money lenders if they didn't fulfill their vow. Shaking your robe or the dust off your feet was a typically Jewish act of condemnation (Acts 13:51; 18:6; Matt. 10:14).

Then the congregation responded with a collective "Amen," which was much more than a Jewish ritual. It was their solemn assent to what had been said and done at the assembly (see Neh. 8:6 and Deut. 27:14ff). The word *amen* means "so be it"; in other words, "May the Lord do all that you said!" It was an act of worship that made the entire assembly a part of the decisions that were made.

Then the congregation unitedly praised the Lord. Why? Because God had enabled Nehemiah to help them begin to solve their problems, and he had directed the money lenders to acknowledge their sins and make restitution. This great assembly was not an "economic summit"; it was a worship service where Nehemiah had lifted a financial problem to the highest possible level. God's people need to follow his example and deal with every problem in the light of the will of God as declared in the Word of God.

3. A great example (Neh. 5:14-19)

D.L. Moody said, "A holy life will produce the deepest impression. Lighthouses blow no horns; they only shine." In our day of public scandals in almost every area of life, especially the political, how refreshing it is to meet a man like Nehemiah who put serving the people ahead of getting gain for himself.

Nehemiah never read Philippians 2:1-13, but he certainly practiced it. During his first term of twelve years as governor, and then during his second term of office (Neh. 13:6-7), he used his privileges for helping the people; he did not use the people to build a kingdom for himself. In that day, most officials exercised their authority in order to promote themselves and protect their personal interests. They had very little concern for the needs of the people. As children of God, our example is Jesus Christ and not the leaders of this world (Luke 22:23-30). "A cross stands in the way of spiritual leadership," writes J. Oswald Sanders, "a cross upon which the leader must consent to be impaled" *(Spiritual Leadership,* Moody Press, 1976; p. 105).

In what ways are these men examples to us? To begin with, Nehemiah and his assistants did not use the official expense account for their household expenses, nor did they tax the people in order to have something to eat. They paid their expenses out of their own pockets and didn't ask to be reimbursed.

The Apostle Paul followed a similar policy with the church at Corinth. He could have accepted support from them, as he did from other churches; but he chose to work with his own hands and preach the Gospel to them "without cost" (1 Cor. 9). Paul did not say that *every* Christian worker should do this, for "the laborer is worthy of his hire" (Luke 10:7; 1 Cor. 9:14). But every Christian should follow Paul's example in having a balanced spiritual attitude toward wealth and ministry. We must be willing to sacrifice personal gain for the spiritual good of others (see Acts 20:33-35 and 1 Sam. 12:3).

It has been said that leaders are people who accept more of the blame and less of the credit, but they are also people who quietly sacrifice so that others might have more.

Nehemiah and his associates not only paid their own bills, but they were also careful not to exploit the people in any way (Neh. 5:15). The servants of previous governors had used their positions for personal gain, perhaps taking bribes from the people and promising to represent them before the governor. For people in places of authority, the temptation to increase wealth and power is always present; but Nehemiah and his friends walked in the fear of the Lord and served honestly.

They were examples in a third way: They all participated in the rebuilding of the wall (v. 16). They were not advisors who occasionally emerged from their ivory towers, but workers who stood with the people in the construction and defense of the city. Jesus said, "I am among you as one who serves" (Luke 22:27, NIV); and Nehemiah and his aides had that same attitude.

Nehemiah was an example in another way: He not only paid for his own food, but he shared what he had with others (Neh. 5:17-18). He regularly fed over 150 guests, both residents and visitors, and he gave them a marvelous meal! (See 1 Kings 4:22-23 for Solomon's daily fare.) It is estimated that this amount of food would meet the needs of over 500 guests, so Nehemiah must have kept "open house" constantly. Or perhaps he shared what was left with the people working on the wall. At any rate, he was generous to others and asked for no reward.

Nehemiah 5:19 indicates perhaps the greatest thing about Nehemiah's service: He did what he did only to please the Lord. This is the fourth of his prayers (1:5ff; 2:5; 4:4), a wonderful expression of worship and humility. He didn't want praise or reward from the people; he wanted only the reward God would give him for his sacrificial service (see 13:14). Some of the people may not have appreciated their leaders as they should, but that didn't upset Nehemiah. He knew that the final assessment would come from the Lord, and he was willing to wait (1 Cor. 4:1-5).

If you are in a position of spiritual leadership, this chapter has some important lessons for you. To begin with, *expect problems to arise among your people.* Wherever you have people, you have the potential for problems. Whenever God's work is prospering, the enemy sees to it that trouble begins. Don't be surprised when your people can't always get along with each other.

Second, *confront the problems courageously.* "There is no problem so great that you can't ignore it" might be a good philosophy for a character in a comic strip, but it won't work in the Lord's service. Every problem that you ignore will only go underground, grow deeper roots, and bear bitter fruits. Pray for God's help and tackle the problem as soon as possible.

Third, *be sure that your own integrity is intact.* A guilty conscience will rob you of the spiritual authority you need to give proper leadership, but every sacrifice you have made will give you the extra strength you need to defeat the enemy.

Finally, *see in every problem an opportunity for the Lord to work.* Solving problems in ministry is not an intellectual exercise but a spiritual experience. If we depend on the wisdom of the world, we will get what the world can do; but if we depend on the wisdom of God, we will get what God can do. All that we say and do must be motivated by love, controlled by truth, and done to the glory of God.

The work had been interrupted by the calling of the assembly and the solving of the economic problems, and now it was time for everybody to get back to his or her place on the wall. But Nehemiah's enemies would also be busy. This time they would aim their ammunition especially at Nehemiah and try to defeat him with four devilish devices.

SIX

We Have Heard the Enemy,
and He Is a Liar

Under Nehemiah's gifted leadership, the people completed the rebuilding of the walls. Now all that remained to do was the restoration of the gates and the strengthening of the community within the walls. Since Sanballat and his friends had failed miserably in their attempts to stop the people from working, they decided to concentrate their attacks on Nehemiah. If they could eliminate him, or even discredit him, they could mobilize their allies living in Jerusalem (Neh. 6:17-18) and take over the city.

The average person doesn't realize the tremendous pressures and testings that people experience day after day in places of leadership. Leaders are often blamed for things they didn't do and criticized for things they tried to do. They are misquoted and misunderstood and rarely given the opportunity to set the record straight. If they act quickly, they are reckless; if they bide their time, they are cowardly or unconcerned. Referring to the pressures of leadership, President Harry Truman wrote in *Mr. Citizen,* "If you can't stand the heat, get out of the kitchen!"

People in places of *spiritual* leadership not only have the pressures that all leaders face, but they must also battle an

71

infernal enemy who is a master deceiver and a murderer. Satan comes either as a serpent who deceives or a lion who devours (2 Cor. 11:3; 1 Peter 5:8), and Christian leaders must be alert and spiritually equipped to oppose him. It behooves God's people to pray earnestly, not only for those in *civil* authority (1 Tim. 2:1-3), but also for those in places of *spiritual* authority. If Satan can defeat a Christian leader, he can cripple a whole ministry and discredit the cause of Christ.

The enemy's main purpose was to generate fear in the heart of Nehemiah and his workers (Neh. 6:9, 13-14, 19), knowing that fear destroys faith and paralyzes life. Adolph Hitler wrote, "Mental confusion, contradiction of feeling, indecisiveness, panic; these are our weapons." Both Jesus (Luke 13:31-37) and Paul (Acts 21:10-14) had to face the specter of fear, and both overcame it by faith.

Nehemiah didn't listen to the enemy's lies. He and the people completed the wall and hung the gates in only fifty-two days, much to the chagrin of their adversaries (Neh. 6:15-16). Satan used four strategies in attacking Nehemiah, strategies that he still uses against spiritual leaders today.

1. Compromise: "We will help you work" (Neh. 6:1-4)
Up to this point in the building program, Sanballat, Tobiah, and Geshem (Gashmu, v. 6) *opposed* everything that the Jews did; but now they offered to *cooperate* and help the Jews build the wall. They offered to meet Nehemiah in a village halfway between Jerusalem and Samaria, a quiet place where they could make plans on how to work together. "We're willing to meet you halfway," was their approach. "Now, don't be an unfriendly neighbor!"

Of course, the enemy's strategy was, "If you can't whip 'em, join 'em—and then take over!" Once the enemy gets a foothold in a ministry, he starts to weaken the work from within; and ultimately, the work will fail. While cooperation in the Lord's work is a noble thing, leaders must take care that they cooperate with the right people at the right time for the right purpose; otherwise they may end up cooperating with the enemy. Satan is a master deceiver and has his servants ready to join hands with God's people so he can weaken their hands in the work (2 Cor. 11:13-15).

Loving compromise and cooperation can be good and useful things *if there are no moral or spiritual issues involved.* Happy compromise can invigorate a marriage or strengthen a ministry (Phil. 2:1-4), but this is compromise among people who love each other and have the same purposes in mind. When you invite the devil to join your team, expect him to change the rules and the goals; and expect to be defeated.

Nehemiah rejected their offer because of three convictions. First, he knew that they were lying and wanted to kill him (Neh. 6:2). Nehemiah had the kind of spiritual discernment that leaders must possess if they are going to detect the enemy's strategy and defeat it. Second, he was convinced of the greatness of the work God had given him to do (v. 3). If Nehemiah allowed himself to be distracted and detoured from the work God had called him to do, where would his people go for leadership? A leaderless project is an aimless project and eventually falls apart. Leaders must be good examples and stay on the job.

During over forty years of ministry, as I have watched Christian leaders come and go, I have tried to take Paul's admonition to heart: "Therefore let him who thinks he stands take heed lest he fall" (1 Cor. 10:12, NKJV). I have noticed that when leaders become well-known, they often face the temptation to neglect their God-given work, join the "evangelical jet set," and start speaking all over the country or the world. Before long, the work at home starts to suffer, and often the leader's marriage and family suffer with it; and the enemy gets a foothold. Unless some radical changes are made in priorities, the result is tragic for both God's people and God's work.

This is not to say that Christian leaders must never leave home to minister elsewhere, for they are a gift to *the whole church* and not just to one work (Eph. 4:11-12). But when "the wider ministry" is more exciting than the work at home, leaders must beware; for the enemy is at work. Dr. Oswald J. Smith used to say, "The light that shines the farthest will shine the brightest at home."

Behind these two convictions was a third conviction: The Jews had nothing in common with Sanballat and his crowd, so there could be no basis for cooperation. Nehemiah had made that clear at the very outset of the project when he said to Sanballat, Tobiah, and Geshem, "But as for you, you have no share in Jerusalem or any claim or historic right to it" (Neh. 2:20, NIV). God's people are different from the people of the world and must maintain their separated position (2 Cor. 6:14–7:1). If Nehemiah had cooperated with Sanballat and his allies, how could he have led the nation to separate itself from the foreigners in the land? (Neh. 9:2; 10:28; 13:3) He would have been inconsistent.

Nehemiah had both discernment and determination: He refused to be influenced by their repeated offers (6:4; see 4:12). If their offer was wrong the first time, it would be wrong the fourth time or the fiftieth time; and there was no reason for him to reconsider. Decisions based only on *opinions* might be reconsidered, but decisions based on *convictions* must stand unless those convictions are changed. Otherwise, decision becomes indecision; and the leader who ought to be a guidepost becomes a weather vane.

2. Slander: "We'll tell everybody about you" (Neh. 6:5-9)
The fifth time the enemy approached Nehemiah, it was with an open letter accusing him of sedition. They had hinted at

Jewish insurrection before the project had even begun (2:19), perhaps borrowing the idea from the people who had stopped the building of the temple years before (Ezra 4). Even our Lord was accused by His enemies of promoting sedition (Luke 23:1-5). It would be considered a serious charge in Nehemiah's day, because Persian kings tolerated no resistance from their subjects. Any hint of rebellion was immediately and ruthlessly put down.

It's interesting to see how often the enemy used *letters* in their attacks against the work (Neh. 6:5, 17, 19). An "open letter" to a royal governor would be both intimidating and insulting. Letters to officials were rolled up and secured with seals so that only those with authority could open and read them. Sanballat *wanted* the public to know the contents of the letter because he hoped to undermine Nehemiah's reputation and authority. If some of the Jewish workers believed what was in the letter, Sanballat could organize them and create division within the ranks. It was a splendid opportunity for the enemy to divide and conquer.

Statements like "it's been reported" and "they say" have caused trouble in many local churches and other ministries. In every organization, there are gossip-mongers, hovering like vultures, just waiting for tidbits of slander that they can chew, swallow, and then regurgitate. An anonymous wit has defined *gossip* as news you have to hurry and tell somebody else before you find out it isn't true!

"I would rather play with forked lightning, or take in my hands living wires with their fiery current," said A.B. Simpson, founder of the Christian and Missionary Alliance, "than speak a reckless word against any servant of Christ, or idly repeat the slanderous darts which thousands of Christians are hurling on others, to the hurt of their own souls and bodies."

Not only did his enemies falsely accuse Nehemiah of fomenting a rebellion, but they also said he was planning to

75

make himself king and had prophets prepared to announce his coronation (v. 7). If this report got back to the Persian king, there would be immediate reprisal; and that would be the end of the Jerusalem project.

Christian leaders must know how to handle false accusations, vicious letters, unfounded press reports, and gossip. Otherwise, these devilish weapons will so upset them that they will lose their perspective and spend so much time defending themselves that they will neglect their work. Nehemiah didn't make that mistake. He simply denied the reports, prayed to God for strength, *and went back to work*. He knew that his character was such that no honest person would believe the false reports. If we take care of our character, we can trust God to take care of our reputation.

On more than one occasion, Bible teacher G. Campbell Morgan was the target of savage gossip that accused him of unfaithfulness to the Christian faith. His usual approach was to say, "It will blow over. Meanwhile, I go quietly on with my work." Nehemiah would have approved of his approach.

3. Threats: "We will protect your life" (Neh. 6:10-14)
Shemaiah, a hireling prophet (v. 12), devised a clever plan for trapping Nehemiah. He shut himself up in his house and gave the impression that, like Nehemiah, his life was in danger. When Nehemiah came to see him, Shemaiah suggested that they both take refuge in the temple, where the enemy couldn't reach them (Ex. 21:13-14; 1 Kings 1:50-53). His words were very threatening: "They are coming to kill you; indeed, at night they will come to kill you" (Neh. 6:10, NKJV).

Since he had access to the temple, it's possible that Shemaiah was of priestly descent; but even this didn't influence Nehemiah's decision. He quickly detected the hoax and let it be known that he was not about to run away in the face of danger. In the first place, he was not that kind of a leader.

"Should such a man as I flee?" he asked (v. 11). He had previously said, "I cannot come down!" (v. 3) and now he declared, "I will not go in!" (v. 11) Nehemiah was a true shepherd and not a hireling like Shemaiah (John 10:12-13). If he had run away and hidden in the temple, it would have ruined his reputation forever.

Nehemiah rejected Shemaiah's proposal because it was contrary to the Law of Moses. It was forbidden for a layman to go beyond the altar of burnt offering at the temple. "The outsider who comes near shall be put to death" (Num. 18:7, NKJV). When King Uzziah tried to invade the holy precincts, God smote him with leprosy (2 Chron. 26:16-21). Nehemiah knew that Shemaiah was a *false* prophet because the message he delivered was contradictory to the Word of God (Deut. 13:1-5 and 18:20-22). "What saith the Scripture?" (Rom. 4:3) must be the test of any message, even if that message comes from somebody who claims to be one of God's servants. "To the law and to the testimony: if they speak not according to this word, it is because there is no light in them" (Isa. 8:20).

Nehemiah 6:14 indicates that there was a conspiracy against Nehemiah among the prophets, including a prophetess named Noadiah. This created a great deal of pressure for Nehemiah, for the Jews had great respect for their prophets. Nehemiah was outnumbered, yet he stood his ground. He was a layman opposed by a body of "professionals," yet he refused to give in. He prayed about them and left the matter with the Lord. In verses 9 and 14, we have the fifth and sixth of Nehemiah's "telegraph prayers" that he sent to the Lord in times of crisis. Of course, behind these brief intermittent prayers was a life of prayer that gave them strength.

4. Intrigue: "We will not give up" (Neh. 6:15-19)

The completion of the walls "in troublous times" (Dan. 9:25) was an embarrassment to the enemy, *but they did not give up.*

77

Satan is not a quitter but stays on the field even after it looks as if he has lost the battle. *Many a careless Christian has won the war but afterward lost the victory.* Satan is always looking for "an opportune time" (Luke 4:13, NIV) to attack the victors and turn them into victims. We need to heed the counsel of that saintly Scottish minister Andrew A. Bonar, who said, "Let us be as watchful after the victory as before the battle."

If you can't see Satan working, it's probably because he has gone underground. Actually, we are safer when we can see him at work than when his agents are concealed. Open opposition is good for God's work and God's workers because it keeps us alert and trusting the Lord. "Watch and pray!" was certainly one of Nehemiah's chief admonitions to his people (Neh. 4:9).

It seems incredible that *any* Jew would secretly cooperate with the enemy, let alone Jews who were *nobles* from the royal tribe of *Judah!* If any tribe had a stake in the future of "the city of David," it was the tribe of Judah; for God promised that a Savior and King would come from their tribe (Gen. 49:10; 2 Sam. 7). When these nobles cooperated with Tobiah, they were resisting the Lord, disobeying the Word, and jeopardizing their own future.

Why would they do such a treacherous thing? For one thing, Tobiah wrote them letters and influenced their thinking. Instead of seeking the truth, the nobles believed the enemy's lies and became traitors to their own people. Because they believed he was right, some of the men of Judah even took an oath of loyalty to Tobiah! In his letters, Tobiah no doubt flattered them and made promises to them; and they foolishly believed him. The nobles secretly shared the letters with others, and thus the conspiracy grew.

Don't believe everything you read or hear about Christian leaders. Consider the source and firmly refuse to accept as truth anything that can't be documented. Especially be wary of what the news media say about evangelical leaders; most media people are not too sympathetic with the Gospel. Looking for exciting stories, some reporters will magnify the insignificant into the sensational, while others will lift statements completely out of context. Sad to say, even the religious press is sometimes guilty of this kind of misrepresentation, including some militant publications that have forgotten how to "speak the truth in love" (Eph. 4:15). There are times when you wonder if perhaps we have reached the sad place that Jeremiah wrote about: "Beware of your friends; do not trust your brothers. For every brother is a deceiver, and every friend a slanderer" (Jer. 9:4, NIV).

How could these Jews turn their backs on their own heritage, their own brothers and sisters, and their own God? *The bonds of human connection were stronger than the bonds of spiritual affection.* Because Tobiah was tied to the tribe of Judah through marriage, the nobles of Judah gave the loyalty to him that they should have given to God (Neh. 6:18). The men of Judah forgot that they were "married" to Jehovah God and owed Him their love and loyalty.

But before we criticize these Jewish nobles, let's examine our own lives. Are we totally yielded to the Lord and fully obedient to Him? Do we ever permit human relationships to influence our decisions so much that we deliberately disobey the Word of God? In twenty-five years of pastoral ministry, I have seen more than one professed Christian leave a church fellowship because of something that was done to a relative in the church.

Commodore Josiah Tatnall is an almost forgotten name in American naval history. During the anti-European uprisings in China in 1859, Tatnall came to the aid of a British squadron in the Pei-Ho River and was criticized for it. In his dispatch to the U.S. Secretary of Navy, his defense was simply, "Blood is thicker than water."

That familiar statement was recorded by John Ray in his *English Proverbs* published in 1670; so it's been around for a long time. The meaning is obvious: Humanly speaking, you have greater obligation to a relative than you do to a stranger. But Jesus said, "He who loves father or mother more than Me is not worthy of Me. And he who loves son or daughter more than Me is not worthy of Me" (Matt. 10:37, NKJV). The "blood bond" that unites us to Christ is the strongest bond of all, and our loyalty to Him must come first.

The nobles of Judah weren't satisfied just to get their information and directions from Tobiah, but they felt it necessary to tell Tobiah everything Nehemiah said! No doubt they were hoping to win Tobiah's favor and thus earn a greater reward when Tobiah and his friends took over Jerusalem. In every sense, they were traitors to the nation and to the Lord. Meshullam was one of the workers on the wall (Neh. 3:4, 30), and yet his family was undermining the very work he was doing.

But these traitors went even further: They repeatedly told Nehemiah what a fine man Tobiah really was! "They that forsake the law praise the wicked; but such as keep the law contend with them" (Prov. 28:4). Had the nobles of Judah been studying and meditating on the Word of God, they would have had discernment and not been walking "in the counsel of the ungodly" (Ps. 1:1). They were blinded by lies and flattery and completely out of touch with reality. There was no light in them (Isa. 8:20).

But is the situation much different in churches today? It alarms me the way professed Christians, who claim to be "Bible taught," give their endorsement and support to people who are nothing but religious hucksters. You would think that the recent media scandals would wake people up, but such is not the case. "A horrible and shocking thing has happened in the land: The prophets prophesy lies, the priests rule by their own authority, and my people love it this way," wrote Jeremiah; and then he asked, "But what will you do in the end?" (Jer. 5:30-31, NIV) Indeed, we are facing a day of reckoning. Then what?

Tobiah kept sending letters to his informers, and they in turn kept telling people to change their allegiance before Jerusalem was taken by the Gentiles. Nehemiah ignored the letters and threats and kept on working until the job was completed. After all, his work was "wrought of our God" (Neh. 6:16); and when God begins a work, He completes it (Phil. 1:6).

The story began with "So I prayed" (Neh. 2:4). Then we read, "So I came to Jerusalem" (v. 11). "So they strengthened their hands for this good work" is the next link in the chain (v. 18), followed by, "So built we the wall" (4:6) and, "So we labored" (v. 21).

Now we reach the end of this part of the story: "So the wall was finished" (6:15). But this marks a new beginning, for now Nehemiah must protect what he has accomplished. How he does this is the theme of the rest of the book.

"V" Is for Vigilance

The walls were completed, the gates were restored, and the enemy was chagrined; but Nehemiah's work was not finished by any means. Now he had to practice the truth Paul emphasized in Ephesians 6:13, "And having done all, to stand." Nehemiah had been steadfast in building the walls and in resisting the enemy, and now he had to be steadfast in consolidating and conserving the gains. "Look to yourselves," warned the Apostle John, "that we lose not those things which we have wrought, but that we receive a full reward" (2 John 8).

A city is much more than walls, gates, and houses; a city is people. In the first half of this book, the people existed for the walls; but now the walls must exist for the people. It was time to organize the community so that the citizens could enjoy the quality of life God wanted them to have. God had great things in store for Jerusalem, for one day His Son would walk the city streets, teach in the temple, and die outside the city walls.

This chapter records three important steps that must be taken by any leader in order to protect the people and the work that has been done.

1. Enlisting leadership (Neh. 7:1-3)

Napoleon described a leader as "a dealer in hope," and Nehemiah certainly fits that description. Before the work began, he inspired the people by assuring them that God would prosper their efforts (2:18-20). When the people were afraid, he prayed that God would strengthen them (6:9). When the enemy threatened, Nehemiah stood his ground and called their bluff; and the work was completed in fifty-two days to the glory of God.

Assistants (Neh. 7:2). Like all good leaders, Nehemiah knew he couldn't do the job alone. One of his first official acts was to appoint two assistants, his brother Hanani (see 1:2) and Hananiah, who was in charge of the citadel ("palace"; see 2:8). The citadel was a fortress in the temple area, guarding the north wall of the city, which was especially vulnerable to attack. Hanani and Hananiah would work with Rephaiah (3:9) and Shallum (v. 12), rulers of districts in the city.

Why was Nehemiah convinced that these men would be good leaders? They had two wonderful qualities: They were faithful to God and they feared God (7:2). Dr. Bob Jones, Sr., often said, "The greatest ability is dependability." If we truly fear the Lord, we will be faithful to do the work He has called us to do. When leaders fear people instead of fearing God, they end up getting trapped (Prov. 29:25); and that leads to failure.

Years ago, the German psychiatrist and philosopher Dr. Karl Jaspers said, "The power of leadership appears to be declining everywhere. More and more of the men we see coming to the top seem to be merely drifting." My former "boss" in Youth for Christ International, Dr. Ted Engstrom, wrote in his book *The Making of A Christian Leader* (Zondervan, 1976), "We see the tragedy of weak men in important places — little men in big jobs" (p. 12). British essayist Walter Savage Landor wrote, "When little men cast long shadows, it is a sign that the sun is setting." An ominous statement, indeed!

Not everybody is called to be a Nehemiah, but some of us can be Hananis, Hananiahs, Rephaiahs, or Shallums, and work with God-given leaders to help get the job done right. God is looking for faithful, God-fearing men and women who will have the courage and conviction to serve Him, come what may.

Gatekeepers (Neh. 7:1, 3). What good are strong new gates if nobody is guarding them and controlling who enters and leaves the city? What good are walls if the gates are open to every foe who wants to enter the city? I understand that the Great Wall of China was penetrated by the enemy at least four times, and each time the guards were bribed. Gates and walls are only as good as the people who guard them.

The gatekeepers ("porters" in v. 1) were given specific instructions as to when to open and close the gates (v. 3). To open the gates early in the morning would only invite the enemy to come in while the city was asleep and unprepared. To close and lock the gates without the guards on duty might give enemy agents opportunity to slip in unnoticed.

Guards. Nehemiah also had appointed two kinds of guards ("watches" v. 3): Those to patrol the walls at specific stations and those to keep watch near their own houses. Since many of the people had worked on areas of the wall near their homes (3:10, 23, 28-30), Nehemiah now challenged them to guard the areas they had built. With guards at the gates, watchmen on the walls, and a solid "neighborhood watch," the city was safe from outside attack.

All of this has a message for us today. *If God's people don't protect what they have accomplished for the Lord, the enemy will come in and take it over.* Paul's admonition must be heeded: "And having done all, to stand" (Eph. 6:13). What a tragedy that schools that once were true to the faith are today denying the faith, and churches that once preached the Gospel now have in their pulpits ministers who preach "another gospel." *Every Christian ministry is one short generation away from destruction, and God's people must be on guard.*

We need guards at the gates, faithful men and women who will not allow false Christians to get in and take over the ministry (2 Cor. 11:13-15). We need watchers on the walls to warn us when the enemy is approaching. Christian parents need to guard their homes lest the enemy gets in and captures their children. It is while God's servants are asleep and overconfident that the enemy comes in and plants his counterfeits (Matt. 13:25), so we must be awake and alert.

In this day when "pluralism" is interpreted by most people to mean "agree with everybody about everything and don't make waves," Christians need to remember that they are *different* and must test everything by the Word of God. There are many religions, but there is still "none other name under heaven given among men, whereby we must be saved" (Acts 4:12). Anything that changes that message or weakens our motivation to get that message out is of the devil and must be opposed. We need guards at the gates and watchers on the wall, or the enemy will take over.

2. Establishing citizenship (Neh. 7:4-69)
This section parallels Ezra 2:1-64. If you compare the two lists, you will see that some of Nehemiah's names and numbers differ from those recorded nearly a century before when the exiles returned from Babylon. This does not suggest that there are either errors or contradictions in the Bible. Errors in spelling names or copying numbers could easily creep in over a century, and none of these differences affects any matter of doctrine or duty.

Furthermore, the scribes who kept the public records certainly updated them after the community was established in

Jerusalem. Ezra 2 lists the names of those who set out with Ezra, but it's possible that others joined the group after Zerubbabel's list was completed. For instance, Ezra 2:2 lists only *eleven* leaders, while Nehemiah 7:7 gives *twelve* names, adding Nahamani. "Nehum" in Nehemiah 7:7 is probably "Rehum" in Ezra 2:2. Variations such as this one are to be expected in ancient documents.

Reading this long list of difficult names might be boring to the modern student, but these people were God's "bridge" from the defeats of the past to the hopes of the future. These Jews were the "living link" that connected the historic past with the prophetic future and made it possible for Jesus Christ to come into the world. Ezra 2 and Nehemiah 7 are to the Old Testament what Hebrews 11 is to the New Testament: a listing of the people whose faith and courage made things happen.

Our modern cities are ethnic "melting pots"; but in Jerusalem at that time, the important thing was to be a Jew *and be able to prove your ancestry.* Genealogies were "lifelines" that linked the Jews not only to the heritage of the past but also to their hope for the future. Not to be able to prove your ancestry meant second-class citizenship and separation from all that God had given to Israel (Rom. 9:4-5). Nehemiah wanted to populate the holy city with citizens who knew they were Jews and were proud of it.

There are ten different groups listed here, starting with the *leaders who returned with Zerubbabel (Neh. 7:7).* These twelve men may have represented the twelve tribes of Israel, even though ten of the tribes had been assimilated by the Assyrians when the Northern Kingdom was captured in 722 B.C. The "Nehemiah" mentioned here is not the author of this book, since these men lived nearly a century before. It appears that these were the elders of the people who helped Zerubbabel, the governor, establish the nation.

Next are listed the various *families* or *clans (vv. 8-25)* and the number of people in each family who returned to the land. Verses 27-38 list the people according to their *villages.* It is interesting that the largest group in the entire list came from Senaah (v. 38), a town whose location is a mystery to us. It must have been a large community if nearly 4,000 people came from there. The Hebrew word means "hated," and some students think it refers to a category of citizen and not to a place. These may have been the "lower classes" in the Jewish society. Whoever they were, they worked on the walls (3:3) and helped restore the city.

It is worth noting that these returned exiles had maintained their identification with their native towns and villages. They knew where they came from and were not ashamed of it! Many people in our modern mobile population care little about family roots or even civic loyalty. Home is wherever one's work is, no matter where your original roots were planted. Also, in spite of their local loyalties, these Jews put the good of Jerusalem first (Ps. 137:1-6). True patriotism sees no conflict between loving one's home city and loving one's nation, for both are gifts from God.

The temple personnel are listed next: *priests (Neh. 7:39-42), Levites (v. 43), temple singers (v. 44), gatekeepers (v. 45), and various temple servants (vv. 46-60).* In the original return to the land, it was necessary for Ezra to send for Levites to serve in the restored temple (Ezra 8:15-20). Were the Levites so comfortable in Babylon that they were unwilling to serve in Jerusalem?

The temple servants ("Nethinim") had been organized by David to assist in the temple (Neh. 7:20) and may have been either prisoners of war or descendants of the Gibeonites (Josh. 9:22-27), who relieved the Levites of heavy routine tasks, like cutting wood and drawing water. "Solomon's servants" (Neh. 7:57) were also foreigners who labored for the king. That these non-Jews were willing to leave the secure life in Babylon for the difficulties of life in Jerusalem may indicate that they had come to trust the God of Israel. On the other hand, perhaps they were compelled to return by their masters.

The *singers* will play an important role in the life of the city. There are at least eighteen references to singers in the Book of Nehemiah and eight references to giving thanks to the Lord. There was not much singing during the exile, when the nation was out of fellowship with God (Ps. 137); but now they needed the musicians to maintain worship at the temple.

One group of people, including some priests, *could not prove their genealogies (Neh. 7:61-65)*. For the priests, this would mean being cut off from the temple ministry and the income it provided from the tithes and offerings of the people. But the Law of Moses made it clear that only those whose family line was clearly in the family of Aaron could minister at the altar. Finally, there was a miscellaneous assembly of over 7,000 *servants (v. 67)*. Since the total number of the congregation was over 42,000 (v. 66), about one-sixth of the population was in servitude. Jewish masters must have been very kind to their servants for so many of them to want to travel with them to Judea.

The animals were mentioned (vv. 68-69) because they were vitally important to the Jewish agricultural economy and to the work of rebuilding the nation.

The total of the figures in this list is 29,818; but Nehemiah's total is 42,360. When you add the 7,337 servants and the 245 singers to the 29,818 total, you get a total of 37,400, a difference of almost 5,000 from Nehemiah's figure. Some of these extra unnumbered people may have been priests who could not prove their genealogy (vv. 63-65), as well as others who didn't fit into any special category. If we knew all the facts about how Ezra 2 and Nehemiah 7 were compiled and copied, we would understand these seeming discrepancies.

The important thing is not to count the people but to realize that *these people counted.* In leaving Babylon, they did much more than put their names on a list. They laid their lives on the altar and risked everything to obey the Lord and restore the Jewish nation. They were "pioneers of faith" who trusted God to enable them to do the impossible.

Before we leave this section, it might be good for you to ask yourself, "If I had to prove my genealogy in order to get into God's city, could I do it?" You are heading for one of two destinies—heaven or hell—and only those who belong to God's family can enter heaven. You enter God's family by receiving Jesus Christ as your own Savior, and this alone guarantees your entrance into heaven (John 1:11-12; 3:16; 14:6).

3. Encouraging worship (Neh. 7:70-73)

Citizenship and leadership together can make a state, but it takes worship to make that state into a godly nation. John Stuart Mill wrote, "The worth of a state, in the long run, is the worth of the individuals composing it." But the worth of the individual depends on his or her relationship to God, and this involves worship. If individual godliness declines, the morality of the nation declines.

The parallel passage is Ezra 2:68-70, which tells us that some of the Jewish leaders gave generously to the temple ministry. But Nehemiah informs us that the governor ("Tirshatha") and some of the common people also gave offerings to the Lord. It was only right that the leaders set the example. A thousand drams (Neh. 7:70) would be 19 pounds of gold, and 20,000 drams (vv. 71-72) would be about 375 pounds. It seems obvious that some of the Jewish leaders left Babylon very wealthy men, with precious metals and servants; but within a few years, the economy failed and the nation was in the grips of a crippling depression (Hag. 1).

But all of this money would have been useless were it not for the God-appointed ministers at the temple: the priests, Levites, singers, and helpers (Neh. 7:73). Moses had assigned special towns for the priests and Levites to live in (Num. 35:1-8; Josh. 21), but later Nehemiah had to move some of them into Jerusalem (Neh. 11:1-2).

It was now the seventh month (Oct.–Nov.), when Israel was expected to celebrate the Feast of Trumpets, the Day of Atonement, and the Feast of Tabernacles (Lev. 23:23-44). There could have been no better time for Nehemiah to call the people together to honor the Word of God, confess their sins, and dedicate themselves and their work to the Lord. What began with *concern (Neh. 1)* led to *construction (chaps. 2–3)* and *conflict (chaps. 4–7);* and now it was time for *consecration (chaps. 8–12).*

As we serve the Lord, we must always do our best; but without His help and blessing, even our best work will never last. "Unless the Lord builds the house, they labor in vain who build it; unless the Lord guards the city, the watchman stays awake in vain" (Ps. 127:1, NKJV). Nehemiah knew that there was a desperate need for the people to come back to the Lord and turn away from their secret sins that were grieving Him. Even though Nehemiah was the official representative of a pagan king, he did everything he could to glorify the God of Israel.

One of the key lessons we can learn from this long chapter is that *people are important to God.* When God wanted to take the next step in His great plan of redemption, He called a group of Jews to leave the place of exile and return to their own land. He gave them encouragement from the prophets and leadership from people who feared God and wanted to honor Him. The Lord didn't send a band of angels to do the job; He used common people who were willing to risk their futures on the promises of God.

Today, God is still calling people to leave their personal "Babylons" and follow Him by faith. The church is living in a day of reproach (Neh. 2:17), and there are "ruins" all around us that need to be rebuilt. "If the foundations be destroyed, what can the righteous do?" David asked (Ps. 11:3). The answer is plain: *The righteous can rebuild what has been torn down and start over again!* If you think that an enemy victory is final, then you have lost your faith in God's promises. There is always a new beginning for those who are willing to pay the price.

This chapter also reminds us that *God keeps accounts of His servants.* He knows where we came from, what family we belong to, how much we gave, and how much we did for Him. When we stand before the Lord, we will have to give an accounting of our lives before we can receive our rewards (Rom. 14:7-12); and we want to be able to give a good account.

A third lesson we must learn is that *the Lord is able to keep His work going.* The first group of Jewish exiles left Babylon for Judea in 538 B.C. and, in spite of many difficulties and delays, rebuilt the temple and restored the worship. Eighty years later, Ezra and another group returned; and fourteen years after that, Nehemiah arrived and rebuilt the walls and gates. During the days of Zerubbabel, God raised up the Prophets Haggai and Zechariah to give God's message to His people. No matter how discouraging the situation might be, God is able to accomplish His purposes if we will trust Him and do His will. John Wesley was right when he said that God buries His workers but continues His work. We must not be discouraged!

Finally, and most important, we must all be sure that *we know we are in the family of God.* No matter how much they argued or protested, the priests without legitimate genealogies could not enter the temple precincts and minister at the altar. God is not impressed with our first birth; what He wants is that we experience a second birth and become His children. If you are not certain of your spiritual genealogy, read John 3:1-18 and 1 John 5:9-13 and make sure that your name is written down in heaven (Luke 10:20).

The People and the Book

French author Victor Hugo said over a century ago, "England has two books, the Bible and Shakespeare. England made Shakespeare but the Bible made England." Supporting that view, historians tell us that Elizabethan England was indeed a country of one book, and that book was the Bible.

When they arrived in America, the Pilgrim Fathers brought with them that same reverence for the Word of God. "The Bible came with them," said American statesman Daniel Webster, "and it is not to be doubted that to the free and universal reading of the Bible is to be ascribed in that age that men were indebted for right views of civil liberties." President Woodrow Wilson said, "America was born to exemplify that devotion to the elements of righteousness which are derived from the relevations of Holy Scripture."

Whether the Bible is "making" any nation today may be debated, but one thing is sure: The Scriptures helped to "make" the nation of Israel. They are a "people of the Book" as no other nation has been, and the church today would do well to follow ancient Israel's example. When God's people get away from loving, reading, and obeying the Word of God, they lose the blessing of God. If we want to be like fruitful

95

trees, we must delight in God's Word (Ps. 1:2-3).

This explains why Nehemiah called for a "Bible conference" and invited Ezra the scribe to be the teacher. The walls were now finished and the gates were hung. The *material* needs of the city had been met; now it was time to focus on the *spiritual* needs of the people in the city. Chapters 8–13 of the book record that spiritual ministry: instructing the people (chap. 8), confessing sin (chap. 9), dedicating the walls (chaps 10–12), and cleansing the fellowship (chap. 13).

It is important to note that *Ezra and Nehemiah put the Word of God first in the life of the city.* What happened in Jerusalem from that point on was a by-product of the people's response to the Scriptures. "The primary task of the church and of the Christian minister is the preaching of the Word of God," said Dr. D. Martyn Lloyd-Jones. "The decadent periods and eras in the history of the church have always been those periods when preaching had declined" *(Preaching and Preachers,* pp. 19, 24). The Spirit of God uses the Word of God to cleanse and revive the hearts of the people of God.

If God is to work in and through His people, then they must respond positively to His Word; and this chapter describes three basic responses: understanding the Word (8:1-8), rejoicing in the Word (vv. 9-12), and obeying the Word (vv. 13-18). The whole person — mind (understanding), heart (rejoicing), and will (obeying) — must be captive to God's truth.

1. We must understand the Word of God (Neh. 8:1-8)
The Bible is not a "magic book" that changes people or circumstances because somebody reads it or recites it. *God's Word must be understood before it can enter the heart and release its life-changing power.* Note that six times in this chapter you can find "understanding" mentioned (vv. 2-3, 7-8, 12-13). Only those people old enough to understand the

Scripture were permitted to be in the assembly (v. 3). In our Lord's "Parable of the Sower" (Matt. 13:1-9, 18-23), the emphasis is on understanding the Word of God. Jesus compared understanding and receiving the Word to the planting of seed in the soil, where it takes root and bears fruit.

Ezra was the ideal man to conduct this outdoor Bible school. He was a priest and scribe who "had prepared his heart to seek the law of the Lord, and to do it, and to teach in Israel" (Ezra 7:10). He had come to Jerusalem about fourteen years before Nehemiah had arrived and had already sought to bring the people back to the ways of the Lord (Ezra 7–10).

That the leaders chose the Water Gate for the site of the assembly is interesting. In the Bible, water for washing is a picture of the Word of God (John 15:3; Eph. 5:26), while water for drinking is a picture of the Spirit of God (John 7:37-39). When we apply the water of the Word to our lives, then the Spirit can work and bring the help we need. It is refreshing to the soul when you receive the Word and allow the Spirit to teach you.

Notice the various ministries that Ezra performed for the people during that special conference.

He brought the Book (Neh. 8:1-4). This was on the first day of the seventh month, which was the Jewish equivalent of our New Year's Day. The seventh month was a special time in the Jewish calendar because the Jews celebrated the Feast of Trumpets on the first day, the Day of Atonement on the tenth day, and the Feast of Tabernacles from the fifteenth day to the twenty-first day (Lev. 23:23-44). It was the perfect time for the nation to get right with the Lord and make a fresh new beginning.

The Book that Ezra brought was "the Book of the Law." This was probably the entire scroll of the Torah, the five Books of Moses, the very foundation of the Jewish religion and civil law. It isn't likely that Ezra read and explained all five Books of Moses in that short a time. Perhaps he concentrated on explaining Deuteronomy and referred to the other books as he had need.

Ezra stood on a wooden platform ("pulpit") above the people so they could see and hear him better. He faced the public square where the people stood, and the wall and gate behind him may have served as a sounding board to help project his voice to the vast assembly. In verse 4, he named thirteen men who stood with him, perhaps leaders representing the tribes. Thirteen more men are named in verse 7 along with the Levites; perhaps they were teaching priests.

He opened the Book (Neh. 8:5-6). When Ezra lifted the scroll and unrolled it to the passage he would read, the people who were seated in the square honored the Word of God by standing up. They knew they would not be hearing a mere man speak his own ideas; they would be hearing the very Word of God (1 Thes. 2:13). The people remained standing while the Law was read and explained (Neh. 8:7). Ezra started his reading and teaching early in the morning and continued through midday (v. 3), which means the congregation stood and listened for five or six hours; and this continued for a week (v. 18). No doubt from time to time, he gave the people opportunities to rest; but the people were there to hear God speak and were willing to stand and listen.

After he opened the Word, "Ezra blessed the Lord, the great God" (v. 6). In many churches, there is a blessing *after* the reading of the Scripture; but there is certainly nothing wrong with praising the Lord for His Word *before* we read and hear it. The people affirmed his words by saying "Amen, Amen" (see 5:13), which means "So be it!" It was a united congregation (8:1) that honored the Scriptures and was willing to devote half of their day to hearing it read and taught. They didn't worship the Book; they worshiped the Lord who spoke to them from the Book.

Our churches today have a desperate need in their public services to show more respect for the Word of God. We are commanded to "give attention to the public reading of Scripture" (1 Tim. 4:13, NASB); and yet in many churches, the only Scripture publicly read is the text of the sermon. "Independent churches" criticize "liturgical churches" for being bound to tradition, but the so-called "liturgical churches" at least devote themselves to a systematic public reading of the Word of God. (The word "liturgy" simply means "a form of public worship." *Every* church has a liturgy, either a good one or a bad one.) We wonder how the Holy Spirit feels when He sees Bibles put on the church floor, or used as portable filing cabinets for miscellaneous papers, or even left behind in church where they are stacked up and finally given to the local city mission. We will *defend* the Bible as the Word of God, but we don't always *treat* it like the Word of God.

We are also in too big a hurry to have the meeting end. In some parts of the world, especially in Eastern Europe before the collapse of the Communist bloc, believers would stand for hours in crowded churches to hear Bible teaching. In the average Western evangelical church, the shorter the sermon, the better we like it.

He read and explained the Book (Neh. 8:7-8). The common people didn't own copies of the Scriptures, so they were thrilled to hear the Word of God. The word *distinctly* in verse 8 means that the Law was explained to the people in a language they could understand. The Word was translated and expounded in such a way that the people were able to apply it to their own lives. The Hebrew language would have undergone some changes since the days when Moses wrote the Pentateuch, and the everyday conversational Hebrew of the people would be different in some ways from ancient Hebrew. We need new translations of the Bible, not because the Bible changes, but because our language changes.

Suppose you had to use John Wycliffe's Version of the Bible, the oldest version in English. How much of this passage would you understand *if you did not already know it from another version?*

> alle ye that traueilen & ben chargid come to me & I schal fulfille you. take ye my yok on you & lerne ye of me for I am mylde and meke in herte: and ye schulen finde rest to youre soulis/ for my yok is softe & my charge liyt.

Wycliffe's translation goes back about 600 years (1382); but between Moses' writing of the Law and Ezra's reading of the Law, a thousand years had elapsed!

The Levites assisted Ezra in teaching the Law (v. 7), for this was one of their God-given ministries (Deut. 33:10; Mal. 2:7). They probably mingled with the people and, when there was a break in the reading, answered questions and told them how to apply the Law to their own lives. Here we have a balance between the public proclamation of the Word in the large assembly and the personal application in the smaller groups. Both are important.

2. We must rejoice in the Word (Neh. 8:9-12)

As Ezra read and explained the Word, the assembly's first response was one of conviction and grief. They mourned over their sins, "for by the law is the knowledge of sin" (Rom. 3:20). The law can't save us; it can only convince us that we need to be saved and then point us to Jesus Christ the Savior (Gal. 3:24). The Jews had just observed the annual Day of Atonement, and the Lord had dealt with their sins (Lev. 16); so they should have been rejoicing in His forgiveness. On the Jewish calendar, the Feast of Tabernacles (Succoth) follows the Day of Atonement, giving God's people an entire week of happy celebration (23:26-44). The sequence is important: first conviction, then cleansing, and then celebration.

The Word of God brings conviction and leads to repentance, but it also brings us joy; for the same Word that wounds also heals. "Your words were found, and I ate them, and Your word was to me the joy and rejoicing of my heart; for I am called by Your name" (Jer. 15:16, NKJV). "The statutes of the Lord are right, rejoicing the heart" (Ps. 19:8). "Your testimonies I have taken as a heritage forever, for they are the rejoicing of my heart" (119:111, NKJV).

Assisted by the Levites, Nehemiah convinced the people to stop mourning and start celebrating. *It is as wrong to mourn when God has forgiven us as it is to rejoice when sin has conquered us.* The sinner has no reason for rejoicing and the forgiven child of God has no reason for mourning (Matt. 9:9-17). Yes, as God's children we carry burdens and know what it is to weep (Neh. 2:1-2); but we also experience power that transforms sorrow into joy.

The secret of Christian joy is to believe what God says in His Word and act upon it. Faith that isn't based on the Word is not faith at all; it is presumption or superstition. Joy that isn't the result of faith is not joy at all; it is only a "good feeling" that will soon disappear. Faith based on the Word will produce joy that will weather the storms of life.

It isn't enough for us to *read* the Word or *receive* the Word as others expound it; we must also *rejoice* in the Word. "I rejoice at Your word as one who finds great treasure" (Ps. 119:162, NKJV). In Bible days, people sometimes hid their wealth in jars buried in the ground (Matt. 13:44; Jer. 41:8). If a farmer plowing his field suddenly discovered a jar filled with gold, he would certainly rejoice. There are great treasures buried in God's Word, and you and I must diligently "dig" for them as we read, meditate, and pray; and when we find these treasures, we should rejoice and give thanks.

If we read and study the Word of God only from a sense of duty, then its treasures may never be revealed to us. It is the believer who rejoices in the Word, who delights to read and study it day by day, who will find God's hidden treasures. "Blessed is the man who fears the LORD, who finds great delight in his commands" (Ps. 112:1, NIV). "But his delight is in the law of the LORD, and in His law he meditates day and night" (1:2, NKJV).

Do you delight in God's Word? Would you rather have God's Word than food (119:103; Luke 10:38-42), or sleep (Ps. 119:55, 62, 147-148), or wealth? (vv. 14, 72, 137, 162) If you delight in His Word, God will delight in you and share His best blessings with you.

3. We must obey the Word (Neh. 8:13-18)

Obligation and *appreciation* are certainly strong motives for serving the Lord, but *celebration* is even stronger. When we obey the Lord and serve Him because we rejoice in Him, then our service will be a delight and not a drudgery. The old Bible commentator Matthew Henry wrote, "Holy joy will be oil to the wheels of our obedience." To the believer without joy, the will of God is punishment; but to the believer happy in the Lord, the will of God is nourishment (John 4:34). The Jews still had work to do in their city, and they needed the joy of the Lord to give them the strength to do it.

"When I think upon my God," wrote composer Franz Josef Hayden, "my heart is so full that the notes dance and leap from my pen and since God has given me a cheerful heart, it will be pardoned me that I serve Him with a cheerful spirit."

The Day of Atonement was celebrated on the tenth day of the month and the Feast of Tabernacles from the fifteenth to the twenty-first days. This meant that the leaders had just a few days available for getting the word out to the Jews in the surrounding villages that everybody was going to celebrate the Feast of Tabernacles. It is not enough to hear the Word of God; we must obey what it tells us to do (James 1:22-25). The people not only had joy in hearing the Word, but they also had *"great* gladness" in obeying it (Neh. 8:17, italics mine).

During the seven days of the feast, the Jews lived in booths made of branches and usually built on the flat roofs of their houses. It was a time for *looking back* and remembering the nation's forty years of wandering in the wilderness, when the people were homeless and lived in temporary shelters. But the feast was also a time for *looking around* at the harvest blessings from the hand of God. The Lord had given them a good land, and they were never to forget the Giver as they enjoyed the gifts (Deut. 8). The Feast of Tabernacles was also an occasion for *looking ahead* to the glorious kingdom God promised His people Israel (Zech. 14:4, 9, 16-20). It was a week-long festival of joyful praise and thanksgiving, focusing on the goodness of the Lord.

But the celebrating of the feast was not for enjoyment alone; it was also for enrichment and encouragement. "The joy of the Lord is your strength" (Neh. 8:10). The world's joy is temporary and artificial; and when the joy is gone, people are left with even greater weakness and emptiness. But the joy that comes from the Lord is real and lasting and enriches our lives. God doesn't give us joy *instead of* sorrow, or joy *in spite of* sorrow, but joy *in the midst of* sorrow. It is not *substitution* but *transformation.*

Jesus illustrated this truth by the birth of a baby (John 16:20-22). The same baby that gives the mother pain also gives the mother joy! Her pain is not *replaced* by joy but *transformed into* joy. The difficult circumstances of life are "pregnant" with joy, and by faith we must give that joy time to be born.

The Feast of Tabernacles was a time for sending food and

gifts to others, especially to those who were needy. The Jews had found joy in *hearing* the Word of God, but now they found joy in *sharing* the blessings of God. The mind grows by taking in, but the heart grows by giving out; and it is important to maintain a balanced life.

Nehemiah 8:17 does not teach that the nation had ignored the Feast of Tabernacles since the days of Joshua, because that was not so. The feast was celebrated during King Solomon's day (2 Chron. 8:13) and also when the Babylonian exiles had returned to the land (Ezra 3:1-4). It was not the *fact* of the celebration that was so special but *the way* they celebrated, for it appears that everybody participated enthusiastically. Because every family made a booth, some of the people had to move from the houses into the streets and squares of the city. Apparently in previous years, not all the Jews had made booths and lived in them for the week of the feast. They had given only "token" acknowledgment of the feast. Furthermore, the joyful attitude of the people was beyond anything the nation had ever seen. It was truly a week of joyful celebration that brought glory to the Lord.

Ezra continued the "Bible conference" during the entire week of the feast, day by day reading and explaining the Word of God. The combination of joyful fellowship, feasting, and hearing the Word must have strengthened the people greatly. Then the week concluded with a solemn assembly (Num. 29:35), after which the people returned to their regular daily schedules.

Did the blessings of the celebration last? Yes, for a time; but then the people became careless again, and the leaders had to bring them back to the Word of God. But the failure of the people is not an argument against special times of Bible study or celebration. Someone asked evangelist Billy Sunday if revivals lasted, and he replied, "No, neither does a bath; but it's good to have one occasionally!"

From time to time in the history of the church, God's Spirit has burdened people to pray, search the Scriptures, and confess their sins; and from these sincere spiritual exercises, He has seen fit to bring fresh life to His people. It happened in Nehemiah's day, and it can happen again today.

Can God begin with you?

"If My people, who are called by My name, will humble themselves and pray and seek My face and turn from their wicked ways, then will I hear from heaven and will forgive their sin and will heal their land" (2 Chron. 7:14, NIV).

Amazing Grace!

Jehovah God is the main subject of this chapter—who He is, what He does for His people, and what His people must do for Him. This prayer reviews the history of Israel and reveals both the majesty of God and the depravity of man. Israel responded to God's "great kindness" (Neh. 9:17), "great mercy" (v. 31), and "great goodness" (vv. 25, 35) with "great provocations" (vv. 18, 26) that resulted in "great distress" (v. 37).

It is interesting that three of Israel's great "national prayers" are recorded in Ezra 9, Nehemiah 9, and Daniel 9. Behind these prayers is the promise of 2 Chronicles 7:14 as well as the example of Moses when he interceded for the people (Ex. 32–33).

Dr. Arthur T. Pierson said, "History is His story"; and this chapter bears that out. "That men do not learn very much from the lessons of history is the most important of all the lessons that history has to teach," wrote Aldous Huxley; and philosopher George Santayana wrote, "Those who do not remember the past are condemned to relive it." The church today can learn much from the experiences of Israel, if we are willing to humble ourselves and receive the truth.

As you read this prayer, notice that it reveals the greatness of God (Neh. 9:1-6), the goodness of God (vv. 7-30), and the grace of God (vv. 31-38).

1. The greatness of God (Neh. 9:1-6)

The Feast of Tabernacles had ended, but the people lingered to hear more of the Word of God. Feasting had turned to fasting as the Word brought conviction and people started confessing their sins. In most churches today, a six-hour service — three hours of preaching and three hours of praying — would probably result in some requests for resignations; but to the Jewish people in that day, it was the beginning of a new life for them and their city.

When I was a young believer, churches often had two-week evangelistic campaigns; and it was not unusual for city-wide meetings to go for a month or six weeks in the summer. Gradually a change took place as "special meetings" were shortened to one week, then to a weekend; and now they are almost obsolete. In my itinerant ministry, more than once I have been reminded to watch the clock so the service could end on time. We live in the age of the digest and fast-food, and this mentality has invaded our churches. We piously sing, "Take Time to Be Holy," but we aren't willing to pay the price to do it.

God's greatness is seen in the fact that *He receives our worship (vv. 1-5).* True worship involves many elements: hearing the Scriptures, praising God, praying, confessing sin, and separating ourselves from that which displeases God. Each of these elements is recorded in this paragraph.

Worship involves the Word of God, for the Word of God reveals the God of the Word. "The essence of idolatry," wrote A.W. Tozer in *The Knowledge of the Holy,* "is the entertainment of thoughts about God that are unworthy of Him" (p. 11). The better we know the Scriptures and respond to them, the better we will know God and become like Him. Israel was chosen by God to receive His Law (v. 13) and to know His will. Any worship service that ignores the Scriptures will not receive the blessing of God.

In the Scriptures, God speaks to us; and in prayer and praise, we speak to Him. "Stand up and bless the Lord your God!" (v. 5) is a command every true believer wants to obey. God's name is exalted above every name (Phil. 2:9-11), and we should honor it as we praise Him. It should be "exalted above all blessing and praise" (Neh. 9:5).

The people also took time to confess their sins (vv. 2-3) and seek the Lord's forgiveness. The annual Day of Atonement was past, but the worshipers knew that they needed constant cleansing and renewal from the Lord. We must not major on self-examination to the extent that we start ignoring the Lord, but we must be honest in our dealings with Him (1 John 1:5-10). Whenever you see sin or failure in your life, immediately look by faith to Christ and seek His forgiveness; *and keep on looking to Him.* The more you look at yourself, the more discouraged you will become. Focus on His perfections, not your own imperfections.

Finally, the people separated themselves from the world as they drew near to the Lord (Neh. 9:2; Ezra 6:21). Separation without devotion to the Lord becomes isolation, but devotion without separation is hypocrisy (see 2 Cor. 6:14–7:1). The nation of Israel was chosen by God to be a special people, separated from the pagan nations around them. "You are to be holy to Me because I, the Lord, am holy, and I have set you apart from the nations to be My own" (Lev. 20:26, NIV). The Apostle Peter applied those words to Christian believers in the church today (1 Peter 1:15; 2:9-10).

God's greatness is also seen in the fact that *He is God alone (Neh. 9:6a).* The nation of Israel was surrounded by idolatry and the degrading lifestyle that was associated with pagan worship. In his reading and explaining of the Law, Ezra had certainly emphasized the Ten Commandments (Ex. 20:1-17; Deut. 5:6-21), including the first two commandments that declare the uniqueness of God and the wickedness of idolatry. Even today, faithful Jews still recite "The Shema" (6:4-6) as their declaration of faith in the one and only true God.

One of Israel's ministries to the world was to bear witness to Jehovah, the true and living God. Their Gentile neighbors were surprised that the Jews had no idols (Ps. 115). When Israel turned to idols, as they often did, God disciplined them. In His eyes, their idolatry was like adultery (Jer. 3:1-5); for He had been "wedded" to them at Mt. Sinai when He gave them His covenant.

A third evidence of God's greatness is the fact that *He created the universe (Neh. 9:6b)*. "In the beginning God created the heaven and the earth" (Gen. 1:1) is a statement that can be applied only to Jehovah, the God of Abraham, Isaac, and Jacob. Whenever God wanted to encourage His people, He would point to creation around them and remind them that He had made it all (Isa. 40). He used the same approach to remind them of the foolishness of worshiping idols (Isa. 41). To know that our Father in heaven is the Creator of all things is a great source of strength and peace. Idolatry means worshiping and serving the creature and the creation rather than the Creator (Rom. 1:25). "Thus does the world forget You, its Creator," wrote Augustine, "and falls in love with what You have created instead of with You."

God's greatness is seen in the fact of *His providential care for His creation (Neh. 9:6c)*. He did not simply make everything and then abandon it to its own course. He is involved in the affairs of His creation: He sees when a sparrow falls (Matt. 10:29), and He hears when a raven cries out for food (Ps. 147:9). He has the stars all counted and named (v. 4), and He has even numbered the hairs on your head (Luke

12:7). "You open Your hand and satisfy the desire of every living thing" (Ps. 145:16, NKJV).

Finally, God's greatness is seen in the fact that *the hosts of heaven worship Him (Neh. 9:6d).* You and I can't duplicate the mighty works of the angels, but we can imitate their devotion to the Lord as they worship before His throne. *And we have more cause to praise Him than they do!* We have been saved by the grace of God and shall one day be like the Lord Jesus Christ. We are not just servants; we are *children* of God (1 John 3:1-3) and will dwell with Him forever!

In our worship, it's wise to begin with the greatness of God. If we focus too much on what He gives or what we want Him to do, we may find our hearts becoming selfish. Sincere worship honors God in spite of circumstances or feelings or desires.

2. The goodness of God (Neh. 9:7-30)

This prayer rehearses the history of Israel, revealing God's goodness to His people and their repeated failure to appreciate His gifts and obey His will. The word "give" is used in one way or another at least sixteen times in this chapter (KJV), for our God is indeed the "giving God," who delights in meeting the needs of His people (1 Tim. 6:17). God gave Israel a land (Neh. 9:8, 15, 35), a law (v. 13), the ministry of the Spirit (v. 20), food and water (vv. 15, 20), deliverers (v. 27), and victory over their enemies (vv. 22, 24). What more could they want?

Centuries before, Moses had warned the people not to forget God, either His gracious hand of blessing or His loving hand of chastening (Deut. 8). Alas, the nation didn't thank God in times of blessing, but they were quick to turn to God for help in times of suffering (see Pss. 105–106). Let's not be too quick to judge them, because some of God's people today treat God the same way.

111

In my years of pastoral ministry, I have met people who had little interest in God or the church until a loved one was in the hospital or there was a death in the family. Then the pastor and all the church family had to drop everything and give them help! But just as soon as the crisis was over, these people were back to their old life again, ignoring the things of the Lord and living for the things of the world.

You can trace this tragic pattern in every stage of Israel's history.

Forming the nation (Neh. 9:7-18). It was an act of pure grace when God chose Abram and revealed Himself to him, for Abram was an idolater in a pagan city (Josh. 24:2-3). Eventually, God changed his name from Abram ("exalted father") to Abraham ("father of a multitude"), because He had promised to make him a great nation (Gen. 12:1-3; 17:1-8). Though Abraham had occasional lapses of faith, for a century he trusted the Lord and walked in obedience to His will. His obedient faith was made especially evident when he gave his son Isaac on the altar (Gen. 22; Heb. 11:17-19).

God's covenant (Gen. 12:1-3) was the basis for all that God did with and for Abraham and his descendants. It was God's purpose that *all the world* be blessed through Israel, and He did this in the sending of His Son, Jesus Christ (Gal. 3:8). God gave the land to Abraham and his descendants, even though during his lifetime Abraham owned nothing in the land but a cave for burying his dead (Gen. 23).

In the land of Egypt, the nation multiplied greatly, saw God's power over the pagan gods, and experienced deliverance from bondage by the mighty hand of God (Ex. 1–15). God opened the sea to let Israel through and then closed it again to destroy the Egyptian army. It was complete deliverance; Israel was to have no further relationship with Egypt.

God led His people by day and by night, giving them food to eat and water to drink. He also gave them His holy Law, so that in their civil, personal, and religious life, they knew the will of God. The Sabbath was given as a special sign between God and His people (Ex. 31:13-17), but there is no evidence in Scripture that the Sabbath law was given to any of the Gentile nations.

In Nehemiah 9:16-18, Nehemiah tells us how the nation responded to all that God had done for them: They refused to bow to His authority ("hardened their necks"), listen to His Word ("hearkened not"), or obey His will. At Kadesh-Barnea, they tried to take matters in their own hands and appoint a new leader to take them back to Egypt (v. 17; Num. 14:1-5). When Moses was on the mountain with God, the people made and worshiped an idol (Neh. 9:18; Ex. 32). Moses interceded for the people, and God pardoned them.

How could these people turn their backs on God after all He had done for them? *They did not truly love Him.* Their obedience was only an outward form; it didn't come from their hearts. In their hearts, they were still living in Egypt and wanting to return there. They did not have a living faith in God but were willing to receive His help and enjoy His gifts. Read Psalm 78 for an "x-ray" of Israel's spiritual history.

Leading the nation (Neh. 9:19-22). During the forty years of Israel's discipline in the wilderness, the old generation died and a new generation was born; but God never forsook His people. He led them by the cloud and fire, taught them the Word, provided them with the necessities of life, and gave them victory over their enemies. God keeps His promises and fulfills His purposes. If we obey Him, we share in the blessing; if we disobey Him, we miss the blessing; but God's purposes will be fulfilled and His name glorified.

Like too many of God's people today, the Jews were shortsighted: They forgot the glorious purposes that God had in mind for the nation. Had they meditated on God's promises and purposes (Gen. 12:1-3; Ex. 19:1-8), they would not have wanted to go back to Egypt or mingle with the godless nations around them. Israel was a people who lived beneath their privileges and failed to accept fully God's will for their lives.

Chastening the nation (Neh. 9:23-30). God promised to multiply His people, and He kept His promise (Gen. 22:17). He also promised to give them a good land, and He kept that promise (13:14-18; 17:7-8). Under the leadership of Joshua, the army of Israel invaded Canaan, conquered the land, and claimed all its wealth. It was God who gave them victory and enabled them to possess cities, houses, lands, and wealth in the land of Canaan.

It was a "fat land" ("fertile," NIV), and Israel became a "fat people" (nourished, satisfied); and this led to their downfall. "But Jeshurun [Israel] grew fat and kicked; you grew fat, you grew thick, you are covered with fat; then he forsook God who made him" (Deut. 32:15, NKJV). Moses' warnings went unheeded (Deut. 8). Israel delighted themselves in God's great goodness *but they did not delight themselves in the Lord.* Like the prodigal son (Luke 15:11-24), they wanted the Father's wealth but not the Father's will.

"For every one hundred men who can stand adversity, there is only one who can stand prosperity," said Thomas Carlyle. Novelist John Steinbeck wrote, "If you want to destroy a nation, give it too much—make it greedy, miserable and sick." It's possible for a local church to get proud of its "riches" and become poor in God's eyes (Rev. 3:14-22). The church that we may think is poor is probably rich in God's eyes (2:8-9).

"Give me neither poverty nor riches," prayed Agur the wise man. "Feed me with the food You prescribe for me; lest I be full and deny You, and say 'Who is the LORD?' Or lest I be poor and steal, and profane the name of my God" (Prov.

30:8-9, NKJV). Through the power of Christ, Paul had learned by experience "how to be abased" and "how to abound" (Phil. 4:12); and that is the lesson all of God's people need to learn.

Once in the land, Israel enjoyed rest during the days of Joshua and the elders who had served with him; but when those godly leaders were gone, the new generation turned away from the Lord (Jud. 2:6-15). God disciplined them, so they cried out for help; and God raised up deliverers to rescue them. Then they would walk in God's ways for a time, lapse back into sin; and the cycle would be repeated. The Book of Judges records the sad story of how God disciplined His people *in their own land* by allowing their pagan neighbors to rule over them.

Against the dark background of Israel's unfaithfulness shines the bright light of the faithfulness of God. When Israel obeyed Him, He was faithful to bless; when they disobeyed Him, He was faithful to chasten; when they asked for mercy, He was faithful to forgive. God is willing to give His people many privileges, but He will not give them the privilege of sinning and having their own way. God's purposes are more important than our pleasures, and He will accomplish His purposes even if He has to chasten us to do it.

Israel's sins finally became so disgusting to God that He decided to discipline them *away from their own land.* He used the Assyrians to destroy the Northern Kingdom, and then He brought the Babylonians to take the Southern Kingdom (Judah) captive and to destory Jerusalem and the temple. It was as though God said to His people, "You enjoy living *like* the heathen so much, I'll let you live *with* the heathen." The nation's seventy years of captivity in Babylon taught them to appreciate the blessings they had taken for granted, and they never again returned to pagan idolatry.

God's chastening is as much an evidence of His love as is

His bountiful supply of our needs (Heb. 12:1-11). We should be grateful that God loves us too much to allow us to become "spoiled children." *The Father is never as close to us as when He is chastening us.* "Blessed is the man You discipline, O Lord, the man You teach from Your law; You grant him relief from days of trouble, till a pit is dug for the wicked" (Ps. 94:12-13, NIV). "Before I was afflicted, I went astray; but now have I kept Thy Word" (119:67).

3. The grace of God (Neh. 9:31-38)

God was good to His people when His people were not good to Him. He sent them prophets to teach them and to warn them, but the nation refused to listen (2 Chron. 36:14-21). He was merciful to forgive them when they cried out for help, and He was long-suffering with them as they repeatedly rebelled against His Word. He could have destroyed the nation and started over again (see Ex. 32:10 and Num. 14:11-12), but He graciously spared them. In His mercy, God didn't give them what they deserved; and in His grace, He gave them what they didn't deserve.

As the Levites prayed, they acknowledged the sins of the nation and God's justice in sending punishment. "In all that has happened to us, you have been just; you have acted faithfully, while we did wrong" (Neh. 9:33, NIV). Note that the Levites used the pronoun "we" and not "they." As they prayed, they identified with the nation and acknowledged their own guilt. Nehemiah had prayed the same way at the beginning of the book (1:6-7). It is easy to be convicted about other people's sins, but God forgives only when we repent and confess our own sins.

In the past, although the nation had enjoyed abundant blessings, they still sinned against the God who had blessed them. Now those blessings had been taken away from them. They were back in the land, but they could not enjoy the land; for everything they worked for was given to somebody else! The Persian king was in control of everything, including their own bodies.

When God had been their king, the Jews had enjoyed great blessing; but when they rebelled against His will, they found themselves enslaved to kings who had no compassion on them. Samuel had warned them (1 Sam. 8), and Moses had prophesied that the nation would forfeit its wealth to its conquerors (Deut. 28:15ff). *Whatever we fail to give God, we cannot keep for ourselves. He will take it one way or another.* Christians who refuse to honor God joyfully by faithful giving often end up having to spend that money reluctantly on obligations that are painful and unexpected, like doctor bills or home repairs (see Mal. 3:7-12).

The Levites had acknowledged God's greatness and goodness; and now, on the basis of His grace, they asked Him for a new beginning for the nation. They couldn't change the servitude they were in, but they could surrender themselves to a greater Master and seek His help. No matter who exercises dominion over us, if we are yielded to the Lord, we are free in Him (1 Cor. 7:22; Eph. 6:5-9). If God had been merciful to Israel in the past, forgiving their sins when they cried out to Him, would He not be merciful to them now?

But they did more than ask God for mercy; they also made a solemn covenant with God to obey His law and do His will. The nation had made a covenant with God at Mt. Sinai and then broken it (Ex. 24:3-8). They had renewed the covenant when they entered Canaan (Josh. 8:30-35) and after they had conquered the land (24:14-28), but then they rebelled against the Lord (Jud. 2:6-15).

Samuel had led the people in renewing their covenant vows (1 Sam. 11:14–12:25), but King Saul led the people back into sin and defeat. As soon as his throne was secure, David sought to bring the people back to the Lord (2 Sam. 6); and

Solomon's prayer at the dedication of the temple was also a step in that direction. Sad to say, however, Solomon sinned against the Lord and almost destroyed his own kingdom.

Throughout the history of Israel, there was always a remnant of faithful people who trusted God, obeyed His will, and prayed for God to fulfill His promises (1 Kings 19:18; Isa. 1:9; Luke 2:38). This believing remnant was God's "lifeline" to maintain the ministry of Israel in the world. They kept the light of faith and hope burning in the land; and because of them, God was able to fulfill His promise and bring the Savior into the world. The Jews in Jerusalem in Nehemiah's day were a part of that remnant, and God heard their prayers.

Our God is a glorious God (Neh. 9:5). He is powerful (v. 6), faithful (v. 8), and concerned about the needs of His people (v. 9). He is a pardoning God (vv. 17-19, 31), who is long-suffering when we sin (vv. 21, 30) but who chastens if we rebel (vv. 26ff). He is a generous God (vv. 24-25, 35), who gives us far more than we deserve. He is a God who keeps His promises even if we are unfaithful.

Surely this God deserves our loving obedience!

Perhaps the time has come for a new beginning.

T E N

After We Say "Amen"

The story may be apocryphal, but it illustrates the point that this chapter makes.

In a certain church, there was a man who always ended his prayers with, "And, Lord, clean the cobwebs out of my life! Clean the cobwebs out of my life!"

One of the members of the church became weary of hearing this same insincere request week after week, because he saw no change in the petitioner's life. So, the next time he heard the man pray, "Lord, clean the cobwebs out of my life!" he interrupted with, "And while you're at it, Lord, *kill the spider!*"

It's one thing to offer the Lord a passionate prayer of confession, such as we have in chapter 9, and quite something else to live an obedient life after we say "Amen." But the people in the assembly were serious about their praying and were determined, by God's grace, to make a new beginning and live to please the Lord.

"The victorious Christian life," said Alexander Whyte, "is a series of new beginnings." The Lord is able to keep us from stumbling (Jude 24); but if we do stumble, He is able to lift us up and get us going again. "The steps of a good man are

119

ordered by the Lord, and He delights in his way. Though he fall, he shall not be utterly cast down; for the Lord upholds him with His hand" (Ps. 37:23-24, NKJV). The nation had sinned, but now it was taking new steps of dedication and obedience.

But was their dedication real? There are at least three evidences given in this chapter that these people really meant what they prayed. These same evidences will be seen in our lives if our promises to the Lord are sincere.

1. Submission to the Word of God (Neh. 10:1-27, 29)

With Nehemiah's name heading the list, eighty-four persons put their seal on the covenant that they made with the Lord. This list included priests (vv. 2-8; see 12:1-7), Levites (10:9-13), and the leaders of the people (vv. 14-27). Many other citizens subscribed to the covenant who didn't "sign their names" individually (v. 28), including wives and children who didn't have the legal right to put a personal seal on an official document. All the people who had heard the Word of God read and explained were now committing themselves to obey what they had heard.

Putting a seal on this document was a serious matter because it meant taking a solemn oath before the Lord (v. 29; see 5:13). Perhaps they had heard Ezra read this passage from Deuteronomy: "All of you stand today before the Lord your God: your leaders and your tribes and your elders and your officers, all the men of Israel, your little ones and your wives . . . that you may enter into covenant with the Lord your God, and into His oath, which the Lord your God makes with us today, that He may establish you today as a people for Himself, and that He may be God to you, just as He has spoken to you, and just as He has sworn to your fathers, to Abraham, Isaac, and Jacob" (Deut. 29:10-13, NKJV).

The law governing vows and oaths is found in Numbers 30

and is introduced with these words: "When a man makes a vow to the Lord or takes an oath to obligate himself by a pledge, he must not break his word but must do everything he said" (v. 2, NIV). Since an oath involved the name and possible judgment of God, it was not to be taken lightly. Jesus warned against using empty oaths (Matt. 5:33-37; 23:16-22), and Solomon gave a similar warning (Ecc. 5:1-7).

Should believers today bind themselves with oaths as they seek to walk with the Lord and serve Him? Probably not. Our relationship to the Lord is that of children to a Father, and our Father wants our obedience to be based on love. I don't know of any examples in the New Testament of believers taking oaths of obedience to the Lord. Our obedience should be a joyful response to all that He has done for us in Christ (Col. 3:1ff). We don't succeed as Christians because we make promises to God, but because we believe the promises of God and act upon them. Oaths are often based on fear ("I had better do it or God will judge me!"), and fear is not the highest motivation for godly living, although it does play a part (2 Cor. 7:1).

2. Separation as the people of God (Neh. 10:28, 30-31)
The Jewish remnant was surrounded by idolatrous Gentiles, who wanted the Jews to become a part of their social, religious, and business society. But the Law of Moses prohibited God's people from living like the Gentiles, although it didn't stop the Jews from being good neighbors or even good customers (see 13:15-22). It was the ministry of the priests to teach the people "the difference beween the holy and the common and show them how to distinguish between the unclean and the clean" (Ezek. 44:23, NIV).

Separation is simply total devotion to God, no matter what the cost. When a man and woman get married, they separate themselves from all other possible mates and give them-

selves completely to each other. It is total commitment motivated by love, and it is a balanced decision: We separate *from*
others *to* the one who is to be our life's mate.

The Jews separated *from* the peoples around them and *to*
the Lord and His Word (Neh. 10:28; 9:2). They also united
with their brothers and sisters in promising to obey the Law
of God (v. 29). Separation that ignores God and other believers is *isolation* and will eventually lead to sin. Only the Holy
Spirit can give us the kind of balance we need to live a godly
life in this ungodly world. The legalist wants to live by rules,
but that style of life only keeps you immature and dependent
on your spiritual leaders. The only way to grow in a balanced
life is to give yourself totally to God and follow Him by faith.

Two special areas of concern were mentioned: marriage
and the Sabbath. The danger in mixed marriages was the loss
of faith on the part of the Jewish mate (Ex. 34:10-17). How
could a Jew, married to a Gentile, observe the dietary laws or
celebrate the annual festivals? He or she would be continually
ceremonially unclean. Between the husband and wife there
would be constant conflict, then occasional compromise, and
finally complete conformity; and the Jewish mate would have
abandoned his or her spiritual heritage.

Why would Jews want to marry pagan Gentiles in the first
place? Apart from affection, which should have been controlled at the outset, perhaps they would marry for social
status (Neh. 13:28) or to get ahead in business. Like some
believers today who marry unbelievers, these Jews may have
argued that marriage would give them opportunity to convert
their mate to the true faith, although it is usually the other
way around. God had a great purpose for Israel to fulfill, and
the Jews' compromise with sin polluted the nation (Mal. 2:10-
16). God wanted a "pure seed" so that through Israel He
could send His Son into the world to be the Savior, and mixed
marriages only brought confusion.

"As long as we love each other, it will work out!" is the argument many pastors hear from Christians who want to marry unsaved people. But the question is not, "Will this marriage work out?" but, "Will this marriage enjoy God's best blessing and fulfill God's will?" It's difficult to see how God can bless and use people who deliberately disobey His Word (2 Cor. 6:14–7:1; 1 Cor. 7:39).

The observance of the Sabbath was a distinctively Jewish practice (Neh. 9:14; Ex. 20:8-11; 30:12-18); the Gentiles around Jerusalem would treat the seventh day of the week like any other day and want to socialize and do business. While the Jewish Sabbath was not to be a day of bondage and misery, it was a day devoted to rest and contemplation of things spiritual. It was a weekly reminder to the nation that they were Jews and had a special calling in the world. Some of the Jewish merchants would be especially interested in getting business from the Gentiles, and to close up business on a day when people were shopping seemed a waste.

Moses didn't spell out specific rules for observing the Sabbath, but there was a precedent for not engaging in unnecessary work. They were not to light any fires on the Sabbath (Ex. 35:1-3), and one man was stoned because he gathered wood on the Sabbath (Num. 15:32-36). The prophets sternly rebuked the Jews for violating the Sabbath (Jer. 17:19-27; Amos 8:4-6; Isa. 56:1-2; 58:13-14), because their disobedience was a symptom of a deeper spiritual problem: rebellion against the Lord.

The solemn affirmation of faith reported in this chapter also included observing the Sabbatical Year (Lev. 25:1-7, 20-22; Deut. 15:1-11). Every seventh year, the Jews were to let the land lie idle so that it might restore itself, an excellent principle of ecology. Of course, the people would need a great deal of faith to trust God for food for two years; but God promised to care for them. After seven Sabbatical Years, they were to celebrate the fiftieth year as a "Year of Jubilee" (Lev. 25:8ff); and this meant trusting God for food for *three* years.

The evidence is that the nation had not faithfully celebrated these special Sabbatical observances. This was one reason why God sent them into Captivity (2 Chron. 36:21), that He might give the land seventy years of rest (Jer. 29:10). This would compensate for some 500 years of disobedience on the part of the nation (7 x 70), one year for each neglected Sabbatical Year or Year of Jubilee.

For the Jewish remnant to promise to commemorate the Sabbatical Year was a great step of faith, for many of the people were poor and the nation faced repeated agricultural and economic depression. Not to have extra produce for a whole year would certainly affect their business with the Gentiles around them. The people's willingness to obey this law is a beautiful illustration of Matthew 6:33.

3. Their support for the house of God (Neh. 10:32-39)
The phrase "house of our God" is used nine times in this section and refers to the restored temple. The people were promising God that they would obey His laws and provide what was needed for the ministry at the temple. "We will not forsake the house of our God" (v. 39).

British expositor G. Campbell Morgan said: "Whereas the house of God today is no longer material but spiritual, the material is still a very real symbol of the spiritual. When the Church of God in any place in any locality is careless about the material place of assembly, the place of its worship and its work, it is a sign and evidence that its life is at a low ebb" *(The Westminster Pulpit,* vol. 8, p. 315).

Morgan is right. To be sure, God doesn't live in the houses in which we assemble to worship Him (Isa. 60:1-2; Acts 7:48-50), but the way we care for those buildings indicates what we think of our God (see Hag. 1). The restored Jewish temple didn't have the magnificence of the temple Solomon built (Ezra 3:8-13; Hag. 2:1-9), but it was God's house just the same and deserved the support of God's people.

Their promised support was specific and involved four different areas of ministry.

The temple tax (Neh. 10:32-33). The annual census of the people twenty years of age and older was accompanied by the collecting of a half-shekel tax to be used to support the ministry of the house of God (Ex. 30:11-16). The tax was a reminder to the people that God had redeemed them and paid a price to set them free, and that they should behave like people who belonged to God. The original tax was used to make silver sockets and hooks for the tabernacle (38:25-28), but in subsequent years it helped pay the expenses of the ministry.

Times were hard, so the leaders decided to adjust the tax and give a third of a shekel instead of a half. (By the time our Lord was ministering on earth, the tax was back to half a shekel; Matt. 17:24-27.) This temporary change didn't alter the meaning of the tradition or lessen the devotion of the people. God's people must use their common sense as they seek to obey the Lord. We must not put on ourselves burdens that God never expected us to carry (Acts 15:10), but neither should we look for the easiest and least demanding way to serve the Lord.

Nehemiah 10:33 describes how the money would be spent: to provide what was needed for the regular and special ministries at the temple, all of which were part of the "work of the house of our God." If the nation was to be in a right relationship with the Lord, the priests had to carry on their ministry faithfully.

We today don't have to provide animals, grain, and other materials in order for the church to worship the Lord; but we do have to help maintain the work of the ministry. This means paying salaries (Luke 10:7), sharing with the needy (1 Cor. 16:1-3), and being good stewards of all that God gives us (2 Cor. 8–9), so that the Gospel may be sent to the whole world. "For where your treasure is, there will your heart be also" (Matt. 6:21). If we are walking with the Lord, we will want to do our part in supporting the ministry of the church where God has put us.

The wood offering (Neh. 10:34). Since the fire on the brazen altar was to be kept burning constantly (Lev. 6:12-13), it required a steady supply of wood; and wood was a precious commodity. The leaders drew lots and assigned the various clans the times when they were to bring wood for the altar. That such a humble thing as wood was important to God's service and could be sanctified for His glory is an encouragement to me. Not everybody in Israel could be a priest or Levite, or donate lambs or oxen for sacrifices, but everybody could bring some wood and help keep the fire burning.

There are no special directions in the Law concerning this offering, but tradition says that certain days of the year were set aside for the people to bring wood to the sanctuary. When God doesn't give us specific instructions, and we know there is a need to be met, we must figure out how to do the job. Since the priests needed wood for the altar, and the people could provide it, an equitable system was worked out.

The firstfruits (Neh. 10:35-37a). The Jews were taught to give God the first and the best, and this is a good example for us to follow today. "Honor the Lord with your wealth, with the firstfruits of all your crops" (Prov. 3:9, NIV). Because God saved the firstborn Jews from death in the land of Egypt, the firstborn of man and beast belonged to the Lord (Ex. 14:1-16; Lev. 27:26-27). The firstborn son had to be redeemed by a sacrifice (Ex. 34:19-20; Luke 2:22-24) because that child belonged to God.

Nowhere does Scripture tell us how much of the firstfruits

the people were to bring to the temple (Ex. 23:19; 34:26), but the offering was to be brought before the people did anything else with their harvests. These were stored for the use of the temple servants (Neh. 12:44). No doubt the offering was to be measured by the blessing God had given to His people, as well as their devotion to Him.

The tithes (Neh. 10:37b-39). The word *tithe* means "a tenth." The Jews were to bring a tenth of their produce to the Lord each year for the support of the Levites (Lev. 27:30-34). The Levites then gave a "tithe of the tithe" to the priests (Num. 18:25-32). The Jews were also to tithe the 90 percent that was left and take it to the temple for the annual feasts (Deut. 26:1-11). To these two tithes was added a third tithe, received every third year for the poor (vv. 12-15; 14:28-29). When the spiritual life in Israel was at low ebb, there was little brought to the temple to support the ministry; and many of the Levites had to find other means of support. In times of spiritual quickening, the people would bring their offerings, and there would be plenty (2 Chron. 31:1-12; Mal. 3:8-11).

While there is no express command in the New Testament that God's people should tithe today, proportionate giving is certainly commended (1 Cor. 16:1-3). We are stewards of God's wealth and must make wise use of what He shares with us (4:1-2). If people under Old Testament Law could bring *three* tithes, how much more ought we to give today who live under the New Covenant of God's abundant grace? (See 2 Cor. 8–9 and note the repetition of the word "grace.") Tithing can be a great blessing, but those who tithe must avoid at least three dangers: (1) giving with the wrong motive, out of a sense of duty, fear, or greed ("If I tithe, God must prosper me!"); (2) thinking that they can do what they please with the 90 percent that remains; (3) giving only the tithe and failing to give love offerings to the Lord.

In light of all that God has done for us, how can we rob

Him of the offerings that rightly belong to Him? God didn't forsake His people when they were in need (Neh. 9:31), and they promised not to forsake the house of God (10:39). Years before, the Prophet Haggai had rebuked the people because they were so busy taking care of their own houses they had neglected the house of God (Hag. 1:4); and this warning needs to be heralded today. *Where there is true spiritual revival, it will reveal itself in the way we support God's work, beginning in our own local church.* It isn't enough to pray or even commit ourselves to "faith promises" or pledges. We must so love the Lord that generous giving will be a normal and joyful part of our lives.

Sir Winston Churchill said, "We make a living by what we get, but we make a life by what we give." Jesus said, "Where your treasure is, there will your heart be also" (Matt. 6:21).

"We will not forsake the house of our God!" (Neh. 10:39)

The Shout Heard 'Round the World

Theologians remind us that God made the first garden (Gen. 1–2), but rebellious man built the first city (4:16-17), and the two have been in conflict ever since. In the ancient world, cities were places of wealth and power. In modern times, in spite of their magnificence, too often our cities are bankrupt institutions famous for pollution, poverty, and crime. How to finance and manage the great cities is a vexing problem to government leaders around the world. "We will neglect our cities to our peril," John F. Kennedy said, "for in neglecting them we neglect the nation."

Nehemiah followed the same philosophy. He knew that the nation of Israel could never be strong as long as Jerusalem was weak. But Jerusalem could not be strong unless the people were willing to sacrifice. Nehemiah calls on the people to present three sacrifices to the Lord for the sake of their city, sacrifices that God still calls His people to give for the sake of the church He is building in this world.

1. We must give ourselves to God (Neh. 11:1–12:26)

Now that the walls and gates of Jerusalem were restored, it was important that the Jews inhabit their capital city and

make the population grow. For one thing, people were needed to protect the city; for they never knew when the enemy
might decide to attack. It may have been safer for the people
to live in the small outlying villages that were no threat to
the Gentile society, but somebody had to take the risk and
move into the big city.

Also, if the people really loved God and their holy city, they
would want to live there, if only as a witness to the skeptical
Gentiles around them. After all, why rebuild the city if you
don't plan to live there? But most of all, God had brought the
remnant back home because He had a special job for them to
do; and to abandon the restored city was to obstuct the working out of God's will through Israel.

In other words, God needed people—live bodies—in the
holy city. The Jews were asked to heed a call not unlike the
one Paul wrote in Romans 12:1: "I beseech you therefore,
brethren, by the mercies of God, that you present your bodies a living sacrifice, holy, acceptable to God, which is your
reasonable service" (NKJV).

Never underestimate the importance of simply being physi-
cally present in the place where God wants you. You may not
be asked to perform some dramatic ministry, but simply *being
there* is a ministry. The men, women, and children who
helped to populate the city of Jerusalem were serving God,
their nation, and future generations by their step of faith.

Some of these citizens volunteered willingly while others
had to be "drafted" (Neh. 11:1-2). The people had promised
to tithe their produce (10:37-38), so Nehemiah decided to
tithe the people; and 10 percent were chosen by lot to move
from the villages into Jerusalem. Since there were few residents in the city and since the housing situation was bad
(7:4), it isn't surprising that many of the Jews were unwilling
to move. We wonder what would happen in the average local
church if 10 percent of the congregation were asked to relo-

cate in order to strengthen and extend the work of the Lord!

We have grown accustomed to Nehemiah's practice of listing the names of the people involved in his projects. In chapter 3, he told us who the people were who worked on the wall and what part of the wall they repaired. Chapter 7 lists the names of the people who returned with Zerubbabel, and chapter 8 records the names of the leaders involved in the "Bible conference" at the Water Gate. Chapter 10 contains the names of eighty-four men who set their seals to the dedication covenant. In listing these names, Nehemiah was giving evidence of his sincere appreciation for each individual who assisted in the work. It also reminds us that our Father sees and records what His children do as they serve Him. Even if others don't recognize or appreciate your ministry, you can be sure that God knows all about it and will reward you accordingly.

The people of Judah and Benjamin who lived in Jerusalem are listed first (11:4-9). These two tribes composed the kingdom of Judah after the nation divided (1 Kings 11–12). "Valiant men" (Neh. 11:6) or "mighty men" (v. 14) can mean "brave fighting men" or "wealthy men of substance," such as Boaz (Ruth 2:1).

The priests, Levites, and temple workers are named next (Neh. 11:10-24). God had set aside special cities for them (Josh. 21), so they could have legitimately lived outside Jerusalem; but they chose to be with the people as they served God in the temple. Like Jeremiah, they chose to remain with God's people, even though it might have been safer and more comfortable elsewhere (Jer. 40:1-6).

A variety of people were needed for the temple ministry that was so important to the Jewish nation. The priests officiated at the altar, and the Levites assisted them. Some supervised the maintenance of the building (Neh. 11:16) while others ministered with prayer and praise (vv. 17, 22); and both were important. There were nearly 300 men appointed to guard the temple (v. 19). Since the tithes and offerings were stored in the temple, it was important that the building be protected. It took many people, with many skills, to maintain the ministry in Jerusalem.

When I was pastor of Calvary Baptist Church in Covington, Kentucky, one Sunday I started listing the people, seen and unseen, who helped make my pulpit ministry possible. While I was preaching, there were three technicians running the controls in the radio room, half a dozen men patrolling the parking lots, ushers at the doors and walking through the buildings to see that all was well, maintenance personnel keeping the equipment going, and an efficient pastoral staff backing me up. The musicians had led the congregation in praise and helped prepare them for hearing the Word.

During the previous week, scores of Sunday School workers had contacted hundreds of people, church members had invited many visitors to the services, the office crew had kept the organizational machinery running smoothly, church officers had encouraged and counseled, people had prayed — and all of this so that the pastor might be able to glorify Christ by proclaiming the Word of God! Believe me, it was a humbling experience; and it made me want to do my best for the Lord and for those wonderful people.

God uses many people with different gifts and skills to get His work done in this world. The important thing is that we give our bodies to the Lord so that He can use us as His tools to accomplish His work. Each person is important and each task is significant. Note that Nehemiah lists other temple ministers in 12:1-26.

In verse 23, Nehemiah states that the king of Persia helped support the ministry at the temple. Since the king wanted the Jewish people to pray for him and his family, he shared in the temple expenses (Ezra 6:8-10; 7:20-24). In our modern democracies, where there is a separation of church and state, this kind of support would be questioned. But the province of Judah was one small part of a great empire, ruled by an all-powerful king; and the king did for the Jews what he did for all the other provinces. Christians today are commanded to pray for civil leaders (1 Tim. 2:1-2; see Jer. 29:7), and this should be done daily and on each Lord's Day when the church assembles to worship.

Pethahiah (Neh. 12:24) was the "king's agent" who represented the Jews at court. People involved in government are God's ministers (Rom. 13:1-7), whether they realize it or not; and if they are faithful, they are serving the Lord just as much as the priests and Levites in the temple.

In Nehemiah 12:25-36, Nehemiah names the villages where the Jews were living, some of which were quite a distance from Jerusalem. When the exiles returned to the land from Babylon, they would naturally want to settle in their native towns and villages. They would still be under the authority of Nehemiah and expected to be loyal to the king of Persia. This loyalty to their native cities was what helped make it difficult for Nehemiah to get people to reside in Jerusalem. While it is good to cultivate local loyalties, we must remember that there are larger obligations that must also be considered. The work of the Lord is bigger than any one person's ministry or the ministry of any one assembly.

2. We must give our praise to God (Neh. 12:27-42)

The Jews were accustomed to having *workers* and *watchers* on the walls of Jerusalem, but now Nehemiah and Ezra assigned people to be *worshipers* on the walls. They conducted a dedication service with such enthusiasm that their shouts and songs were heard "even afar off" (v. 43).

The people had been dedicated (chaps. 8–10); now it was time to dedicate the work that the people had done. This is

133

the correct order, for what good are dedicated walls and gates without dedicated people? Note that the emphasis was on *joyful praise* on the part of all the people. *Singing* is mentioned eight times in this chapter, *thanksgiving* six times, *rejoicing* seven times, and *musical instruments* three times.

The order for the dedication service was unique. The leaders and singers were divided into two groups, with Ezra leading one group and Nehemiah (following the choir) directing the second group. The processions started probably from the Valley Gate on the west wall, marching in opposite directions. Ezra's company (12:31-37) went south on the walls to the Dung Gate, then to the Fountain Gate and the Water Gate on the east wall of the city. Nehemiah's company went north (vv. 38-39) past the Old Gate, the Ephraim Gate, the Fish Gate, the Sheep Gate, and the Muster Gate ("gate of the guard"). Both groups met at the temple area where the service climaxed with sacrifices offered to the Lord.

Why did Ezra and Nehemiah organize this kind of a dedication service? Why not just meet at the temple area, let the Levites sing and offer sacrifices to the Lord, and send everybody home?

To begin with, it was the walls and gates that were being dedicated; and it was only right that the people see and touch them. I recall sharing in a service of dedication for a church educational building; but the service was held in the church sanctuary, not in the educational building. At some point in that service, we should have left the sanctuary and marched through the new building singing praises to God. As I ministered the Word, I felt as though I were performing a wedding for an absentee bride and groom!

But there is another reason for this unique service: The people were bearing witness to the watching world that God had done the work, and He alone should be glorified. The enemy had said that the walls would be so weak that a fox could knock them down (4:3), but here were the people *marching on the walls!* What a testimony to the unbelieving Gentiles of the power of God and the reality of faith. It was another opportunity to prove to them that "this work was wrought by our God" (6:16).

By marching on the walls, the people had an opportunity to see the results of their labors and realize anew that the work had not been done by one person. True, Nehemiah had been their leader, and they needed him; but "the people had a mind to work" (4:6). Various people and families had labored on different parts of the wall (chap. 3), but nobody "owned" the part he or she had worked on. The wall belonged to God.

You can expect serious problems after a church building program if individuals or groups in the church start claiming "territorial rights." I heard about one Sunday School class that actually sued the church when they were asked to vacate their classroom and locate elsewhere in the building. No matter how much work or money we have put into a building program, this does not earn us the right to claim and control some area of the building. *It all belongs to God and must be used for His glory.* As the Jews marched around the walls, they were symbolically saying just that. "Yes, we all had part in the work and a place to serve, but now we are giving it all to the Lord that He alone might be glorified!"

Let me suggest another reason for this march around the walls: It was a symbolic act by which they "stepped out by faith" to claim God's blessing. In that day, to walk on a piece of property meant to claim it as your own. God said to Abraham, "Arise, walk through the land . . . for I will give it unto thee" (Gen. 13:17); and He said to Joshua, "Every place that the sole of your foot shall tread upon, that have I given unto you" (Josh. 1:3). This joyful march around the walls was their way of saying, "We claim from our God all that He has for us, just as our forebearers claimed this land by faith!"

Too often, a church dedication service marks the *end* and not the beginning of ministry as the congregation breathes a sigh of relief and settles down to business as usual. Vance Havner once described his impressions of a dedication service at which he had spoken: "The church people thought the new building was a milestone, but it looked to me like it was a millstone!" If we lose our forward vision and stop launching out by faith, then what God has accomplished will indeed become a millstone that will burden and break us.

But the most important thing about this dedication service was not the march around the walls. It was the expression of joyful praise that came from the choirs and the people. "By Him [Christ] therefore let us offer the sacrifice of praise to God continually, that is, the fruit of our lips, giving thanks to His name" (Heb. 13:15). "I will praise the name of God with a song, and will magnify Him with thanksgiving. This also shall please the Lord better than an ox or bullock that hath horns and hoofs" (Ps. 69:30-31).

The people offered their praise thankfully (Neh. 12:24, 27, 31, 38, 46), joyfully (vv. 27, 43-44), and loudly (vv. 42-43), accompanied by various instruments (vv. 27, 35-36). It was not a time for muted meditative worship. It was a time for "pulling out all the stops" and praising the Lord enthusiastically.

This special service of dedication would have been a failure were it not for a man who had been dead for over 500 years. That man was King David. It was David who had organized the priests and Levites (v. 24; 1 Chron. 24:7-19) and written many of the songs for the temple choirs (Neh. 12:46). He had also devised musical instruments for use in worship (v. 36; 2 Chron. 29:26-27). David had served his generation faithfully (Acts 13:36), but in doing so, he had also served every generation that followed! In fact, it was David who captured the Jebusite city of Jerusalem and made it his capital, the City of

David (2 Sam. 5:6-10). It was also David who had provided the blueprints and much of the wealth for the building of the temple (1 Chron. 28:11-19). "He who does the will of God abides forever" (1 John 2:17, NKJV).

It was not only the "professional musicians" who expressed praise to God, for the women and children also joined in the singing (Neh. 12:43). They had heard the Word at the Water Gate (8:2), so it was only right that they now express their worship; for learning the Word and worshiping the Lord must go together (Col. 3:12). We must never permit the accomplished ministry of worship leaders to take the place of our own spontaneous celebration of the Lord's goodness. Otherwise, we will become spectators instead of participants; and spectators miss most of the blessing.

So great was the people's praise that "the joy of Jerusalem was heard even afar off" (Neh. 12:43). This was now the third time in Israel's history that their shouting was "heard afar off." The soldiers shouted when the ark of the covenant came into their camp (1 Sam. 4:5), but that eventually led to shameful defeat. When the temple foundation was laid nearly a century before, the workers shouted for joy; but their joy was mingled with sorrow (Ezra 3:8-13). The shout from Jerusalem during this dedication service was unalloyed joy, to the glory of the Lord; and because of this record in the Word of God, *that shout has been heard around the world!*

3. We must give our gifts to God (Neh. 12:44-47)
The people had covenanted with God to support the temple ministry (10:32-39), and they kept their promises. Some of the Levites were appointed to supervise the collecting of the produce and the storing of it in the temple. Keep in mind that these tithes and offerings represented the support of the temple workers so that they could serve the Lord.

The people brought their tithes and offerings, not only

because it was the commandment of God, but also because they were "pleased with the ministering priests and Levites" (12:44, NIV). The ministers at the temple were exemplary both in their personal purity and in their obedience to God's Word (vv. 30, 45). They conducted the worship, not according to their own ideas, but in obedience to the directions given by David and Solomon. When believers have a godly ministry that exalts the Lord and obeys the Word, they are only too glad to bring their tithes and offerings to support it. A worldly ministry that seeks only to fulfill its own ambitions does not deserve the support of God's people.

The result of this joyful service of dedication was a plentiful supply of produce to sustain the work of the ministry. The people gave "not grudgingly or of necessity" but joyfully and gratefully (2 Cor. 9:7). Missionary leader J. Hudson Taylor used to say, "When God's work is done in God's way for God's glory, it will not lack God's support."

Our material gifts are really spiritual sacrifices to the Lord, if they are given in the right spirit. The Apostle Paul called the gifts from the Philippian church "an odor of a sweet smell, a sacrifice acceptable, well pleasing to God" (Phil. 4:18). Jesus accepted Mary's gift of precious ointment as an act of worship, and Hebrews 13:16 reminds us that doing good and sharing are sacrifices that please the Lord.

But before we can bring our material gifts to the Lord, we must first give ourselves to Him. Paul commended the churches of Macedonia because they "first gave themselves to the Lord" (2 Cor. 8:5, NKJV), before they shared in the missionary offering he was receiving for the needy believers in Jerusalem. Our gifts cannot be a substitute for ourselves.

It was a high and holy day in Jerusalem, a happy day because the work had been completed and God had been glorified in a wonderful way. Did the blessing last? No, it didn't; and we will find out why in the next study.

T W E L V E

Standing by Our Promises

General William Booth, founder of The Salvation Army, once said to a group of new officers, "I want you young men always to bear in mind that it is the nature of a fire to go out; you must keep it stirred and fed and the ashes removed."

Nehemiah discovered that the fires of devotion had gone out in Jerusalem. His first term as governor lasted for twelve years (5:14), after which he returned to the palace to report to the king (13:6). He was gone perhaps a year; but when he returned to Jerusalem, he discovered that the situation had deteriorated dramatically, for the people were not living up to the vows they had made (chap. 10). Nehemiah immediately began to act decisively to change the situation.

Without spiritual leadership, God's people are prone to stray like sheep. One successful pastor told me, "If we didn't keep our eyes on this work twenty-four hours a day, seven days a week, it would be invaded and soon fall apart." Moses was away from the people of Israel only a short time, and they became idolaters (Ex. 32). Paul would establish a church and leave it in the hands of the elders, only to have trouble begin soon after his departure. Then he would have to write

139

them a letter or pay them a visit to straighten things out. (No wonder Paul exhorted the Ephesian church leaders as he did in Acts 20:28-32!) After Nehemiah was gone from Jerusalem only a short time, he came home to find the people defiled by compromise.

If you compare this chapter with chapter 10, you will see that the people failed to keep several of the promises that they had made to the Lord.

1. The separation promise (Neh. 13:1-9, 23-31)

The mixed multitude (Neh. 13:1-3). According to 10:28-29, the Jews had willingly separated themselves from the people of the land and united with their Jewish brothers and sisters to obey the Law and walk in the way of the Lord. But apparently their separation was incomplete, or some of the people formed new alliances; for they discovered that there were Ammonites and Moabites in their congregation, and this was contrary to the Law of Moses (Deut. 23:3-4).

Ammon and Moab were born from the incestuous union of Lot and two of his daughters (Gen. 19:30-38), and their descendants were the avowed enemies of the Jews. Somehow this "mixed multitude" had infiltrated the people of Israel in spite of previous purgings (9:2; 10:28). It was the "mixed multitude" that gave Moses so much trouble (Ex. 12:38; Num. 11:4-6), and it gives the church trouble today. The "mixed multitude" is composed of unsaved people who want to belong to the fellowship of God's people without trusting the Lord or submitting to His will. They want the blessings but not the obligations, and their appetite is still for the things of the world.

Balaam was a hireling prophet who tried to curse Israel but each time saw the curse turned into a blessing (Num. 22–24). Finally, however, he hit upon a scheme to defeat Israel: He encouraged the Moabites to be "neighborly" and invite the

Jews to share in their religious feasts, which involved immorality and idolatry (Num. 25). Balaam knew that human nature would respond to the opportunity for sin and the Jews would disobey God. As a result of their sin, Israel was disciplined by God, and 24,000 people died.

The "mixed multitude" in the church today urges us to follow the philosophy of Balaam and do what the world wants us to do. I was told about a dedicated youth pastor whose ministry was bringing many teens to Christ and building them up in the faith. He didn't entice them with entertainment; he simply taught the Word, kept the young people busy witnessing, and met with them regularly for prayer. The church was being greatly helped by this group of dedicated teenagers.

But the enemy went to work. The youth pastor was called before the elders and asked, "What is your program for ministering to the carnal young people in the church?" He said that he had no special program for carnal teenagers, but that they were welcome to join in the Bible studies, prayer meetings, and witnessing trips. *The elders dismissed the youth pastor because he was not catering to the carnal teens in the church!*

When I was ministering over "Back to the Bible Broadcast," the manager of a Christian radio station phoned me to complain about my messages about Lot and worldliness among professing Christians. He felt I was being too hard on the carnal Christians. "If you keep that up," he said, "we're going to drop your program!"

The old Youth for Christ slogan is still true: In ministry, we must be "geared to the times and anchored to the Rock." If we understand the times (1 Chron. 12:32), we can relate to people more easily and apply the Word with greater skill; *but we must not imitate the world in order to try to witness to the world.* Years ago, Oswald Chambers wrote, "Today the world has taken so many things out of the church, and the church has taken so many things out of the world, that it is difficult to know where you are" *(The Servant As His Lord,* p. 17). "Today the world has so infiltrated the church," said Vance Havner, "that we are more beset by traitors within than by foes without. Satan is not fighting churches—he is joining them."

An enemy intruder (Neh. 13:4-9). Not only were some of the Jews married to Ammonites or Moabites, but also *an Ammonite was living in the Jewish temple!* Tobiah the Ammonite (4:3) had been given a room in the temple by Eliashib the high priest (13:28). Eliashib is the first one named in the list of workers (3:1), and yet he had become a traitor. Why? Because one of his relatives was married to Sanballat's daughter (13:28), and Sanballat and Tobiah were friends. They were all a part of the secret faction in Jerusalem that was fraternizing with the enemy (6:17-19).

Just because a family has been active in the church a long time and has helped to build the work, it is no sign that each generation will be spiritual, or that any generation will *remain* spiritual. Children and grandchildren can drift from the faith and try to bluff their way on the testimony of their ancestors, and fathers and mothers can depart from the faith just to please their children. Eliashib's relative was privileged to be born into the priestly family, yet he threw away his future ministry by marrying the wrong woman (Lev. 21:14; Deut. 23:3); and Eliashib apparently approved of it.

All this happened while Nehemiah was away at the palace, which suggests that those he appointed to lead in his absence had failed in their oversight. *It doesn't take long for the enemy to capture leadership, and too often the people will blindly follow their leaders in the path of compromise and disobedience.*

It was bad enough that an Ammonite was living in the temple, and that a Jewish high priest had let him in; but this intruder was using a room dedicated to God for the storing of the offerings used by the Levites. He defiled the temple by his presence and robbed the servants of God at the same time. Nehemiah lost no time throwing out both the man and his furniture, rededicating the room to the Lord, and using it again for its intended purpose. Like our Lord, Nehemiah had to cleanse the temple; and it appears that he had to do it alone.

But this is not an easy thing to do. A new pastor may discover officers or leaders in the church who are not spiritual people but who are entrenched in their offices. What does he do? He knows that these leaders have relatives in the church who, like Eliashib, will cooperate with their family rather than contend for the faith. Should the pastor try to "clean house" and possibly split the church? Or should he bide his time, lovingly preach the Word, and pray for God to work? With either approach, the pastor will need courage and faith, because eventually the blessing of the Lord on the Word will arouse the opposition of the "mixed multitude."

Mixed marriages (Neh. 13:23-31). "We would not give our daughters as wives to the peoples of the land, nor take their daughters for our sons!" was the promise the Jews had made to the Lord (see 10:30, NKJV); but they did not keep it. In his survey of Jerusalem, Nehemiah saw women from Ashdod (see 4:7), Ammon, and Moab married to Jewish men; and he heard their children speaking foreign languages. (A child is more likely to learn how to speak from his mother, with whom he spends more time, than from his father who is away from home each day working.) If these children did not know the language of Israel, how could they read the Law or participate in the holy services? If a generation was lost to the faith, what was the future of the nation?

God's people and the people of the world can be identified by their speech. "They are from the world and therefore speak from the viewpoint of the world, and the world listens

143

to them. We are from God, and whoever knows God listens to us; but whoever is not from God does not listen to us. This is how we recognize the Spirit of truth and the spirit of falsehood" (1 John 4:5-6, NIV).

While ministering at a summer Bible conference, I had dinner one evening in the home of the daughter of a well-known Christian musician and her husband. Both of them were able to talk about her father, now deceased, or about music and musicians; but when the conversation turned to the Word and the Lord, they were silent. I wondered if either of them really knew the Lord, or, if they did, if they were on speaking terms with Him. They had no problem talking about the things of the world, but they did not know "the language of Zion."

Nehemiah dealt with the problem by first expressing his horror that such a thing should be done in Israel (Neh. 13:25). In a similar situation, Ezra had plucked his own hair and beard (Ezra 9:3); but Nehemiah plucked the hair of some of the offenders! Ezra had dissolved the mixed marriages (Ezra 10), but Nehemiah only rebuked the offenders and made the people promise that they would not do it again.

Nehemiah also delivered a sermon, reminding the people that Solomon, one of Israel's greatest kings, was ruined by marrying foreign women (Neh. 13:26; 1 Kings 11:4-8). In Solomon's case, his mixed marriages were a threat to the throne and the kingdom; and in Nehemiah's day, mixed marriages even threatened the priesthood. The Law of Moses was clear, but both the priests and the common people had deliberately disobeyed it. Nehemiah then purified the priests and made certain that only those who were qualified served (Neh. 13:30). However, the problem with the priests was not completely settled, for the Prophet Malachi had to deal with disobedient priests in his day (Mal. 1–2).

How important it is that we take a stand for separation

from sin "and having done all, to stand" (Eph. 6:13).

2. The support promise (Neh. 13:10-14)

"We will not forsake the house of our God," was the final statement the Jews made in their covenant with the Lord (10:39). This meant paying the temple tax, providing wood for the altar, and bringing the required tithes and offerings to the priests and Levites (vv. 32-39). Without the faithful support of the people, the ministry at the temple would languish; and the Levites would then scatter to the villages, where they could work the land and survive (13:10).

But when Nehemiah returned to the city, he discovered that the people had failed to keep their promise. (This helps to explain why one of the storage rooms was available for Tobiah.) The priests and Levites were without support and were deserting their work in order to survive. The people ignored the warnings of Moses, "Take heed to yourself that you do not forsake the Levite as long as you live in your land" (Deut. 12:19, NKJV) and "You shall not forsake the Levite who is within your gates, for he has no part nor inheritance with you" (14:27, NKJV; and 18:1-8).

Nehemiah "contended" with them, which means he rebuked the leaders for breaking their promise and disobeying the Law. Before his survey of the city was completed, he also rebuked the nobles of Judah (Neh. 13:17) and the men married to foreign women (v. 25). While the Hebrew word can refer to arguing or even physical combat, it also carries the judicial meaning of "to plead a case." Since Nehemiah presented God's case and defended it from the Law, the offenders had to admit that he was right.

The temple officers in charge of the gifts had forsaken their posts because there was nothing coming in or going out, so Nehemiah "set them in their place" (v. 11; "stationed them at their posts," NIV). He then saw to it that the people brought to God the offerings that rightfully belonged to Him (Mal. 3:7-12). He appointed four men to supervise the treasury and distribute the tithes and offerings. Note that these men represented the priests, Levites, scribes, and laymen; but they all had one thing in common: They were faithful to the Lord. "Moreover it is required in stewards, that a man be found faithful" (1 Cor. 4:2).

When God's people start to decline spiritually, one of the first places it shows up is in their giving. "For where your treasure is, there will your heart be also" (Matt. 6:21). The believer who is happy in the Lord and walking in His will has a generous heart and wants to share with others. Giving is both the "thermostat" and the "thermometer" of the Christian life: It measures our spiritual "temperature" and also helps set it at the right level.

The prayer in Nehemiah 13:14 is the first one recorded since 6:14 and is the seventh of Nehemiah's "telegraph" prayers found in the book. You find three more such prayers in 13:22, 29, and 31. He was in the habit of talking to God as he served Him, a good example for us to follow. He reminded God of his faithfulness and prayed that what he had done would not be blotted out. Nehemiah was not pleading for blessings on the basis of personal merit, because he knew that God's blessings come only because of God's mercy (v. 22). This prayer is similar to the one recorded in 5:19 where Nehemiah merely asked God to remember him and what he had done. He wanted his reward from God, not from men.

Someone asked the American Episcopal bishop Phillips Brooks what he would do to resurrect a dead church, and he replied, "I would take up a missionary offering." *Giving to others is one secret of staying alive and fresh in the Christian life.* If all we do is receive, then we become reservoirs; and the water can become stale and polluted. But if we both receive and give, we become like channels; and in blessing others, we bless ourselves. American psychiatrist Dr. Karl Menninger said, "Money-giving is a good criterion of a person's mental health. Generous people are rarely mentally ill people." Someone wrote in *Modern Maturity* magazine, "The world is full of two kinds of people, the givers and the takers. The takers eat well—but the givers sleep well."

3. The Sabbath promise (Neh. 13:15-22)
When they signed the covenant, the Jews promised not to do business with the Gentiles on the Sabbath Day (10:31); but Nehemiah found the people not only doing business on the Sabbath, but also doing their daily work and carrying unnecessary burdens. The Jewish merchants didn't want to lose the opportunity to make money from the Gentiles, and the Gentiles were quick to make a profit from their Jewish neighbors.

The child of God must choose spiritual wealth rather than material wealth and claim the promise of Matthew 6:33, "But seek first His kingdom, and His righteousness; and all these things shall be added to you" (NASB). Whoever wrote Psalm 119 made it clear that he chose God's Word rather than money (vv. 14, 72, 127, 162). King Saul made the wrong choice (1 Sam. 15), and so did Achan (Josh. 7) and Demas (2 Tim. 4:10).

In one of the churches I pastored, a lovely young couple began to attend with their little boy. Then I noticed that only the mother and son were attending, so I stopped at the home to see what had happened to the father. I learned that he had taken a second job on weekends so he could save enough money to get a better house. The wife confided that they really didn't need the extra money or a new house, but it was her husband's idea, and she couldn't stop him. The tragedy is, the extra money didn't go to a new house; it went to doctors and hospitals. The little boy contracted an unusual disease that required special medicine and care, and the father's extra income helped pay the bill.

I'm not suggesting that every family with a sick child is unfaithful in their stewardship, or that God makes children suffer for the sins of their parents. But I am suggesting that nobody can rob God and profit from it. If our priorities become confused and we start putting money ahead of God, then we must expect to be the losers.

Nehemiah took three steps toward changing the situation. First, he rebuked the Jews who were working and selling on the Sabbath and made them stop (Neh. 13:15). Then, he rebuked the nobles for allowing business on the Sabbath Day, reminding them that the nation's violation of the Sabbath was one cause for their captivity (vv. 16-18; Jer. 17:21-27). Did they want to have more wrath come on the people?

His third step was a very practical one: He ordered the city gates shut on the Sabbath Day. The guards had been willing to open the gates to the Gentile merchants, possibly because they were bribed; so Nehemiah put some of his own servants on duty. He also ordered the Levites to set a good example on the Sabbath and minister to the people.

The Lord's Day, the first day of the week, is not a "Christian Sabbath," because the Sabbath is the seventh day of the week and belonged especially to the Jews. Therefore, the Old Testament laws governing the Jewish Sabbath don't apply to the Lord's Day. But Sunday is a special day to God's people because it commemorates the resurrection of Jesus Christ from the dead as well as the coming of the Holy Spirit at Pentecost. We ought to use the Lord's Day to the glory of the Lord.

More and more, especially in our cities, Sunday has become a day for shopping, sports, and chores around the house. The shopping center parking lot is as full on Sunday afternoons as it is on Saturdays. I once interviewed the manager of a shopping mall and asked him how he felt about being open on Sundays.

"The employees and I would rather stay home," he replied, "but it's a big day for business, especially from people on their way home from church."

In our family, my wife and I tried to follow the simple principle of not doing on Sundays whatever could be done on any other day of the week, things like mowing the lawn, washing the car, shopping, and so on. The home didn't become a prison, but neither did it turn into a circus; and the children didn't seem to suffer for it.

The French agnostic, Voltaire, is supposed to have said, "If you want to kill Christianity, you must abolish Sunday." I'm not sure I agree with him, but I do know that many Christians have killed their joy, witness, and spiritual power by turning Sunday into an ordinary day and not putting Christ first in their week.

Nehemiah closes with two prayers (Neh. 13:29, 31) that God would remember him for his faithful service. His conscience was clear, for he knew he had done everything for the good of the people and the glory of God. There would probably be little appreciation from the people, in spite of his sacrifices; but he knew that God would reward him accordingly.

May those who come behind us find us faithful!

Looking for Leaders

During the French Revolution, a man was seen running down the street after a mob, moving quickly into danger.

"Stop! Stop!" somebody cried out. "Don't follow that mob!"

As the man continued to run, he called back, "I have to follow them! I'm their leader!"

Nehemiah was certainly not that kind of leader. He wasn't afraid of danger, but he was wise in his plans and careful in his decisions. The church today could use leaders like Nehemiah. We have a lot of rubbish to remove and rebuilding to accomplish before the world will believe that our God is real and our message is worth believing.

What are the characteristics of this man that we ought to emulate? Let me list twelve qualities that made Nehemiah a successful leader. As you read, try to think of passages in the Book of Nehemiah that illustrate these qualities.

1. He knew he was called of God

When everything else fails, the call of God will give you the strength and resolution you need to get the job done. At first Moses resisted the call of God, but then he came to realize that God's calling was the greatest assurance of success (Phil. 1:6; 1 Thes. 5:24). Knowing that God had called him was the secret of Jeremiah's perseverance when everything around him was falling apart and his own people were against him. The worker who doesn't have a divine calling to the work is like a house without a foundation or a ship without an anchor, unprepared for the storms of life.

Nehemiah started with a burden for Jerusalem, but the burden was not the call. He wept over the sad condition of the city (Neh. 1:4), but his tears were not the call. It was as he prayed to God and sought divine help that he received a call to leave his relatively easy job and go to Jerusalem to rebuild the walls. Because he knew God had called him, Nehemiah could approach the king and get help; and he could also enlist the help of the Jews in Jerusalem.

Before you quickly move into a place of ministry, be sure God has called you and equipped you for the job. You may not think you can do it, and others may have their doubts; but if God calls you, have no fear: He will see you through.

2. He depended on prayer

The Book of Nehemiah starts and ends with prayer. And in between, Nehemiah oftens sends up quick prayers to heaven and asks for God's help. Nehemiah was the royal governor of the province, with all the authority and wealth of the king behind him; but he depended solely on God to help him finish the work.

The Christian worker who can get along comfortably without prayer isn't getting much done for God and certainly isn't threatening the enemy too much. "To be a Christian without prayer," said Martin Luther, "is no more possible than to be alive without breathing."

Nehemiah faced a gigantic task, a task too big for him but not too great for God. "Do not pray for tasks equal to your powers," said Phillips Brooks. "Pray for powers equal to your tasks." One mark of true spiritual leaders is their honest acknowledgment of their own inadequacy and their humble trust in the power of God.

We have Nehemiah's brief spontaneous prayers recorded in the book, but behind those prayers was a life of prayer as seen in chapter 1. He certainly had a disciplined prayer life; for our "telegraph" prayers accomplish little if our hearts are not in tune with God. Most Christians never realize the hours that leaders must spend in prayer in order to get the job done. "Pray for great things," said evangelist R.A. Torrey, "expect great things, work for great things, but above all, pray." Nehemiah certainly followed that advice.

3. He had vision and saw the greatness of the work

Leadership involves vision, revision, and supervision; but the greatest of these is vision. Leaders must see what others don't see and then challenge others to follow until they do see. "I am doing a great work, so that I cannot come down!" was Nehemiah's testimony (6:3), and he never lost that vision.

It's an old story but it bears repeating. A visitor was watching some men work on a building and began to question them. "What are you doing?" he asked one, who replied, "I'm making ten dollars a day." When he asked a second man the same question, the worker replied, "I'm laying stones in this building." But the third man answered, "Why, I'm building a cathedral!" He was the man with vision.

No matter what God has called you to do, it's a great work because it's part of the building of His church; and that's the greatest work in the world. I have often told people, "There are no small churches and there are no *big* preachers." In God's kingdom, every job is a big job and every servant is nothing apart from faith in the Lord.

If you lose the greatness of a vision, you will begin to cut corners in your work, stop making sacrifices, and start looking for something else to challenge you. Nehemiah realized that what he was doing was far bigger than simply repairing gates and rebuilding walls. He was serving the Lord God of heaven and getting the holy city ready for the coming of the Messiah!

4. He submitted to authority

The call of God is not an invitation to become independent and ignore authority. Nehemiah respected the king and submitted his plans to him for his approval before he went to Jerusalem. He acknowledged what Paul wrote in Romans 13, that the powers that be are ordained of God for our good, and we should submit to them.

Even more, Nehemiah submitted to the authority of the Word of God. He invited Ezra to teach the Law to the people so that they too would obey the will of God. It is a basic rule of life that *those who exercise authority must themselves be under authority.* Nehemiah was a man who was dependable because he was accountable. In recent years, we have seen the sad consequences of religious leaders refusing to submit to authority and be accountable. When you read the Book of Nehemiah, you meet a man whose work prospered because he submitted to God, the Word, and the king.

5. He was organized in his work

Instead of rushing impetuously into the task, Nehemiah secretly surveyed the situation and became acquainted with the facts. He talked with the Jewish leaders privately and told them his plan. There were no press conferences or "pep rallies." He was simply a man willing to wait for God's direction and then act as soon as the way was clear.

After making his plan, he enlisted his workers and sought

154

to give them the same vision for the task that God had given to him. He had a job for everyone to do and a place for everyone to work. He gave recognition to his workers and encouraged them when the going was tough. He gave them a feeling of security even though the situation was dangerous.

Nehemiah's priorities were right: After the wall was finished, he held a "revival service" for the people and then publicly dedicated the walls. He planned his work and worked his plan, and God blessed him.

6. He was able to discern the tactics of the enemy

Every Christian ministry needs an "intelligence department" that keeps its eye on the enemy and recognizes when he is at work. Nehemiah was not fooled by the enemy's offers or frightened by their threats. He could say with Paul, "We are not ignorant of his [Satan's] devices" (2 Cor. 2:11).

In our study, we have noted the various devices the enemy uses to try to stop the work; and every good leader will want to understand them. Leaders must spot the enemy before anybody else does and be ready to meet him quickly and efficiently. Leaders must recognize when Satan comes as a roaring lion or as a serpent, devouring or deceiving.

7. He worked hard

That seems like a trite statement, but it isn't; for one of the secrets of Nehemiah's success was his willingness to sacrifice and work hard. Had he stayed back in the palace, serving the Persian king, he would have enjoyed an easy life. But once he was in Jerusalem, he went to work, he kept working, and he worked hard.

This is what Charles Spurgeon said to the ministerial students at his Pastors' College in London: "Do not be afraid of hard work for Christ; a terrible reckoning awaits those who have an easy time in the ministry, but a great reward is in reserve for those who endure all things for the elect's sake. You will not regret your poverty when Christ cometh and calleth His own servants to Him. It will be a sweet thing to have died at your post, not turning aside for wealth, or running from Dan to Beersheba to obtain a better salary, but stopping where your Lord bade you hold the fort" *(An All Round Ministry,* p. 197).

"The laborer is worthy of his hire" (Luke 10:7), so let's be sure we are laborers and not loiterers. There is no place in the Lord's service for lazy people who give advice while they watch other people work.

8. He lived an exemplary life

Whether it was working on the wall or feeding hundreds of guests, Nehemiah's life was blameless. His full time was devoted to the work, and he didn't permit himself to be distracted. He refused financial support that was legitimately his and instead spent his own money to help others. He identified with the people and stood right with them as together they built the walls.

The enemy would have rejoiced to discover something in Nehemiah's life that would have embarrassed him and hindered the work, but nothing could be found. Not that Nehemiah was sinless, for only Jesus Christ can claim that distinction; but his life was blameless. Paul exhorts us to become blameless and harmless, "children of God without fault in the midst of a crooked and perverse generation, among whom you shine as lights in the world" (Phil. 2:15, NKJV). The first qualification for the pastor (elder, bishop) is that he be "blameless" (1 Tim. 3:2; Titus 1:6).

There is no subsitute for integrity and the good conscience that goes with it. You can face any enemy, listen to any accusation, or confront any misunderstanding if you have integrity and a good conscience. You have nothing to hide and nothing to fear. It is when people start to lead a double life that they get into trouble, for nobody can serve two masters. Hypocrisy leads to further deception, until the deceivers get caught in their own traps. Sir Walter Scott was right when he wrote:

> O what a tangled web we weave
> When first we practice to deceive!

9. He sought to glorify God alone

If Nehemiah had been interested only in promoting himself, he would have stayed in the palace; for there he was honored as the king's cupbearer and had an easy life. Or when he arrived in Jerusalem as the official governor, he would have used his authority to make life easier for himself. He could have "thrown his weight around" and avoided a great deal of sacrifice and toil.

But he did neither of those things. Instead, he came as a servant, identified with the people, and entered right into their trials and burdens and dangers. In this, he was certainly like our Lord Jesus Christ (Phil. 2:1-11).

Nehemiah was burdened because the city of Jerusalem no longer glorified God. It was a reproach. He was concerned because the people living in Jerusalem were an object of scorn to their Gentile neighbors. He determined to remove the reproach and give the Jews in Jerusalem cause to glorify God.

In the building of the walls and the repairing of the gates, God was glorified. In the way Nehemiah and his people confronted and defeated the enemy, God was glorified. In their dependence on the Lord, God was glorified. In the great service of dedication, the Lord was magnified. From beginning to end, the entire enterprise brought glory to the Lord.

I fear that the church today suffers from having too many

celebrities and not enough servants. The praise too often goes to the workers and not to the Lord. Particularly at some religious conventions, there is so much praise given to men that the Lord is left out of the picture completely. *There is nothing good that God will not do for the worker who humbly serves and lets Him have the glory.*

10. He had courage

There is no place for timidity in leadership. Once you know what God wants you to do, you must have the courage to step out and do it. You must be willing to take some risks and occasionally make some mistakes. You must be able to take criticism, be misunderstood, and even be slandered, without giving up. As Harry Truman said, "If you can't stand the heat, get out of the kitchen."

Nehemiah had the courage to live in a dangerous city and confront a subtle enemy. He had the courage to deal with the traitors among his own people and to call the people back to faithfulness to the Lord. He even threw Tobiah out of the temple! While you and I as Christian workers don't have the authority to pluck out beards or forcibly eject unwanted tenants, we need the same kind of courage Nehemiah had when he did those things.

Someone has said that success is never final and failure is never fatal: It's courage that counts. The ancient Greeks thought that courage was the "master virtue," because without courage you could never use your other virtues. No wonder the Spanish novelist Cervantes wrote, "He who loses wealth loses much; he who loses a friend loses more; but he who loses courage loses all."

11. He enlisted others to work

True leaders don't try to do everything themselves. They not only enlist others, but they also create the kind of climate that enables others to become leaders as well. Real leaders aren't afraid to surround themselves with people who can do some things better than they can. Leaders don't feel intimidated by the excellence of others; in fact, they encourage it. Their job is to challenge others to do their best and help get the job done.

In my study of Christian biographies, I've noticed that God has occasionally raised up men and women who were like magnets in the way they attracted potential leaders to them. D.L. Moody was such a man, and so was Paul Rader. Amy Carmichael had this gift, and so did the late Dr. Bob Cook. Leaders develop other leaders, because they know how to discern spiritual gifts and the potential in a life.

12. He was determined

Lech Walesa, the courageous Polish labor leader who became President of his country, said this about leadership: "To be a leader means to have determination. It means to be resolute inside and outside, with ourselves and with others." If anybody lived up to that description, it was Nehemiah.

Be determined! That's one of the key messages of the Book of Nehemiah. President of Wheaton (Ill.) College, Dr. V. Raymond Edman, used to remind his students, "It's always too soon to quit." Like Jesus Christ, Nehemiah set his face like a flint and kept on going (Luke 9:51; Isa. 50:7). Anyone who puts his hand to the plow and looks back is not fit to serve the Lord (Luke 9:62).

I read about a couple of boys who went around their neighborhood looking for jobs shoveling snow. They saw a man shoveling his driveway and asked if they could do the job.

"Can't you see I'm already half finished?" he said.

"That's why we asked," the boys explained. "You see, we get most of our work from people who got started but weren't able to finish."

Nehemiah was determined because the work he was doing was a great work and he was serving a great God. He was determined because the city was in great reproach, and he wanted it to bring great glory to God. He was determined because he was part of a great plan that God had for the world as He worked through the Jewish nation.

The church today needs leaders, men and women and young people who will determine under God to acomplish the will of God, come what may. The church needs leaders who will say with Nehemiah, "I am doing a great work, so that I cannot come down!"

More than anything else, I want to be able to say at the end of my ministry and my life, "I have glorified You on the earth. I have finished the work which You have given me to do" (John 17:4, NKJV).

So, the next time you feel like quitting, remember Nehemiah and stay on the job until the work is finished to the glory of God.

Be determined!